THE A LISTER

REVEALING SECRET STUDY STRATEGIES TOP STUDENTS DON'T WANT YOU TO KNOW

HO KHINWAI

FOREWORD BY ADAM KHOO

THE A LISTER

Copyright © 2014 Ho Khinwai. All Rights Reserved.
The A Lister: 10 Power Strategies Top Students Don't Want You to Know

Managed by: Zen Invest Solutions, www.zeninvest.com

ISBN:9810942540
Paperback: 978-981-09-4254-0
Kindle / E-book: 978-981-09-4255-7

1. Education   2. Learning   3. Memory

www.thealisterbook.com

No sex discrimination. Where the words "man" or "him" are used, they refer to a person who can either be male or female.

No part of this book may be reproduced or transmitted in any form or by any means, electronic or mechanical, including photocopying, recording, or by an information storage and retrieval system - except by a reviewer who may quote brief passages in a review to be printed in a magazine or newspaper - without permission in writing from the publisher.

For bulk purchase of this book, please email:
khinwai@thealisterbook.com

DISCLAIMER
Although the author has made every effort to ensure that the information in this book was correct at press time, the author does not assume and hereby disclaim any liability to any party for any loss, damage, or disruption caused by errors or omissions, whether such errors or omissions result from negligence, accident, or any other cause. The author makes no representation or warranties (express or implied) with respect to the accuracy, applicability or completeness of the contents.

'The Memory Quadrant' & 'Net of Imperfection' are trademarks of Zen Invest Solutions.

FEEDBACK & TESTIMONIALS
We'd love to hear from you. Please send your feedback, suggestions for future publications, media enquiries and testimonials to **khinwai@thealisterbook.com**

FOREWORD
by Adam Khoo

It is a great pleasure to be writing this Foreword for a brilliant young man, Ho Khinwai. Very few books have been written on the topic of study skills and much fewer, have been written by a student himself!

In this book, Khinwai has spilled the beans on how top students today achieve their 'A's consistently, year after year, semester after semester, in an ever-increasingly competitive environment. Khinwai's book is a treasure trove of strategies that will help any student who desires to become an 'A' Lister.

Given my over-a-decade experience in coaching students of all ages, I've always been amazed at the extraordinary things that ordinary human beings can achieve, if they just put their mind to it. In this book, Khinwai guides you through 10 powerful strategies that will immensely help you skyrocket your grades. If you closely follow the strategies in this book, you WILL surprise yourself, and achieve the extraordinary.

This is not a book that will you read once and throw aside. This book is the result of Khinwai's past experiences and keen observations of many a successful student. It is a book with many invaluable strategies that will enable you to achieve the results that you want. Keep it safe, and read it whenever you face "stumbling blocks" in your studies.

Adam Khoo
Executive Chairman, AKLTG
Best-Selling Author of over 17 books, including 'I Am Gifted, So Are You!'
www.akltg.com

Contents

Foreword I

Acknowledgements IV

Introduction 1

My Education Journey 3

How Will This Book Help Me? 5

Who is this Book Written For? 5

What This Book is Not 6

Getting the Most Out of This Book 7

PART 1:
WHY BOTHER STUDYING ANYWAY? 11

    What is Your "Why"? 13

    One Important Thing Your School Probably
    Didn't Tell You About 17

    Two Traits of Highly Successful Students 19

    Demystifying the
    Myths of Getting Good Grades 20

    Your Learning Style 23

PART 2:
REVEALING 10 POWERFUL STUDY STRATEGIES IN EVERY 'A' LISTERS' ARSENAL 25

The Revelation 27

Strategy 1: The Key is In the Keywords 29

Strategy 2: The Memory Quadrant 39

Strategy 3: Manage This, And You Can Manage Anything 55

Strategy 4: Having A Game Plan 63

Strategy 5: Progression, Not Perfection 79

Strategy 6: The Truth About Being Competitive 87

Strategy 7: The Art of Thinking Critically 101

Strategy 8: New Strategies for 21st Century Students 107

Strategy 9: How to Survive Your Finals 125

Strategy 10: Your Most Powerful Tool 139

Being Hungry!!! 149

No One Said It Would Be Easy 149

Afternotes 151

Online Resources & Recommended Reads 152

About The Author 156

Acknowledgements

To God and the Universe, for giving me the strength and courage, and walk me through my darkest times. Thank you for the gift of life you breathe into me each day. I am grateful.

To my parents who have nurtured and supported me through life, given me the comfort and love of a home, and the resources to be an 'A' Lister.

To my business and life mentors who made me see possibility – Peng Joon, Tianyi Lim, Sam Choo, Imran Md Ali, thank you for allowing me to be in your presence and learn from you.

To my other mentors who've greatly inspired me to become the best I can be – Oprah Winfrey, Joel Bauer, JT Foxx, Warren Buffett, Adam Khoo, Robert Kiyosaki.

To my great friends, Siva, Kenogi, Charles Chua, Wesker Ling, Silvester Chua, Glen Tiew, Min Wei, Yizhun, Jay Ng, Ming Yong, Zackefeller Tee, whom I'm blessed to know through my personal journey and have left an impact on me through your words and actions. Your friendship is something I cherish deeply.

To the peeps at NYP Write Stuff, Jaclyn, Hwee Ming, Dedrick, Mr. Santokh, Ginny, Mirrah, Pavani for igniting that writer in me.

To the awesome 'A' Listers whom I am privileged to meet, Nevin Tan, Calwin Lim, Janessa Hoe, El Christine Shin, Ivan Chock, Jay Zou, Wei Cong, Felicia Ng, Winson Quah, Dickson Tang, Javier Aw, Edison Hon, you've inspired me with your perseverance, intelligence and hard work.

To Gerry Robert, James MacNeil and the entire Black Card Books team who've inspired me and gave me the courage to write my own book.

To my team at Zen Invest Solutions – Isabel Ong, Pavani, Ryan Hong, Joanne Goh for having faith in what I do and helping to make this book a reality.

And to Sam Choo again, for your amazing guidance and giving me that push to "publish a book in 60 days".

To my teachers who made a difference – Mr Amos Goh, Mr Peter Lee, Mdm Goh, Mr Anthony Ng, Ms Salmisna, Mrs Lu-Lim.

To local author friends who've inspired me – Ranford Neo, Michael Lum, Neil Humphreys, the authors from *Invest Lah!*, Jack Wong, David Chua.

To Daniel Wong for actively improving student learning and development in Singapore. And, to Sir Ken Robinson for your efforts in championing change in the education landscape so that students of today can cultivate creativity and 'learn' in the truest sense of the word.

And lastly, to you, who have made a wise investment in this book. I believe nothing is impossible. Persist and focus, because I have faith that you'll soon be flying high with the 'A' Listers!

Dedicated to the God, the Universe and all my amazing mentors. Without you, this book would never have seen the light of day.

Also, to my sister Michelle, for being open to the possibility of an unconventional education.

THE A LISTER

Introduction

What is An 'A' Lister?

The 'A' Lister is a term I designed to represent students who have leapfrogged from ordinary to extraordinary territory. 'A' Listers are once students like yourself, wanting those 'A's badly, but try as they might, they just can't seem to get it.

'A' Listers are successes not primarily because they are 'A' students, but mainly because they have successfully broken past their own boundaries they've placed for themselves.

This book is really all about having breakthroughs and fulfilling your desires.

Why I Wrote This Book

This is the essential guide every student who wants to supercharge their academic grades should have in their bag.

I wish I had this handy book to learn from during my days back in school, when I realized how important getting good grades was. We live in a world where paper qualifications are still (unfortunately) how many people judge your intelligence, importance and net worth on first impression by.

I am not the smartest person in the world, in fact, I'm just like any other ordinary student. Over the course of my education journey, I had to cross over many stumbling blocks, challenges and obstacles, and learn the hard way to getting the kind of results I wanted.

This book came about partly because of the many friends and relatives who wanted to know how I "mastered the study game" and achieve my kind of results. Also, I didn't want anyone to face the same frustration and helplessness as I did when I first started getting serious about my studies, hence, this book was written.

This book is not like any other "memory strategies" or "how to study" books written by PhDs, researchers, teachers or tutors.

This is a practical book written for students by a student himself. It's all the tips, skills and strategies I've picked up having been a part of the 'A' Listers, as well as strategies I've found to work for myself over the years of my studying.

This is not a book that you will read and cast aside. It is a manual containing time-tested study techniques and advices which you will refer to over and over again.

Top students don't want you to know this, because these are the exact strategies they have been using to top their class semester after semester, year after year.

For me, I believe in the law of reciprocity. My sharing of this knowledge is my way of gratitude for all the privileges, opportunities and respect I've gotten from getting fantastic grades.

My Education Journey

I come from a typical, traditional Chinese family in Singapore. When I was 6 years old, I started going to school like every other 6 year old kid did.

I remember the first time I got the notice for my new class, my mom announced to me, "Your class is '2J'. I apparently misheard her saying "Your class is 2 days". I couldn't believe my ears, just two days!

So as you can see, even as a child, I wasn't totally looking forward to school and would rather stay at home playing computer games.

I was all along an average student during my primary school years and the first half of my secondary school years. I blended in with the rest of the kids and just did as much as I could in my studies. In Singapore, education is top priority for parents with school-going children. When a kid fails to live up to their parents' standards (which we never do no matter how high the grades are), the kid is sent for extra classes or tuition. And, that was what I got.

Every week without fail, my tutor would come right up to my home and tutor me in Math, Science or Chinese for 2 hours. I always dreaded tuition and my heart would pound wildly in my chest every time the tutor rang the doorbell.

I didn't pay very close attention to studying until I got to around Secondary 2, where my literature assignment received the highest score in the entire class. I felt ecstatic at that point in time, and I wanted more. That was the point where I decided to focus all of my energies into being an "outstanding" student in class.

I experimented with many different ways to remember key facts and details for many of my subjects in school. Some worked, some didn't. I kept the ones that worked and experimented with them so much so that I literally had a whole arsenal of strategies I could use to supercharge my learning.

Eventually, I graduated secondary school with an aggregate score that opened many course choices for my tertiary education adventure. I chose to study a Banking and Finance course in Nanyang Polytechnic (NYP), where I spent my prime years in my current education journey.

In poly, I continued using the strategies that I've discovered and refined along the way and kept this process running throughout my entire 3 years in school. Along the way, I continued to refine all of my strategies and it was truly phenomenal. Using the strategies I am about to reveal to you in this book, I've managed to score 33 As and Distinctions in total and was on the Dean's list for all of the 6 semesters in school. I was selected as the top student for the cohort and received a gold medal for my good work. Besides that, I managed to find time to participate in CCAs and do well in them.

I show you these results not to impress you, but to impress upon you that an average student can become an outstanding student, if you follow the strategies, tips and tricks I'm about to reveal in the book.

THE A LISTER

How Will This Book Help Me?

This book will open your mind to look at studying in a different light. It will change your perception about student competition and how to unlock your brain's potential to the fullest.

This is not a "theory" book, but a practical book with step-by-step guides and simple activities you must complete and repeat religiously in order to become an 'A' Lister.

This book will potentially turn you from an average, typical student to an 'A' Lister, without any more studying than you currently are doing right now.

Some of the strategies presented in this book may or may not work for you, because every student has his own learning style, pace and preference. You don't have to necessarily use all of the strategies; just use the ones you like and are comfortable using, and I guarantee you that you will see a difference.

Who Is This Book Written For?

This book is written for students who are:

- Unable to get above average grades, despite having studied super-duper hard
- Looking to dramatically raise their grades from FAIL to consistent PASS

- Frustrated and desperate, and NEED to learn how to study more effectively and achieve amazing grades
- Students who are already achieving 'A's and want to learn how to study faster, memorize easier and refine their study strategies.

And, not forgetting...

- Parents, who are looking for a way to help their child learn better, be more motivated and score higher in their studies
- Teachers and tutors who want to make a difference in students' lives by imparting them with learning strategies they can take with them for a lifetime

However, please do NOT read my book if you:

- Are a student who wants to stay in your comfort zone and will not take action to make a change
- Are a student who isn't motivated to improve your grades
- Feel that this book is a complete waste of time and money

What This Book is Not

This book is not a rant on how flawed the education system is or what needs to be changed. Much more influential people like Sir Ken Robinson (a great educator whom I greatly admire) have already set the motion for a change in this area.

Rather, this is a book of practical strategies to tackle the nagging problems of students right now in our current

THE A LISTER

education system. That being said, I've also included some cutting-edge concepts that will help you to excel no matter how the system changes.

This book is also not about me. I don't proclaim to be the smartest or the best student out there, just because I've written a book on study skills. I'm here as a messenger, a friend who wants to share with you what 'A' Listers do – what works, what doesn't.

Getting the Most Out of This Book

In the following pages, you'll learn the exact techniques that will help you to unlock your brain potential and supercharge your learning to achieve fantastic grades. You'll also discover the reasons many students study so diligently and fastidiously, yet get a lower grade on a test or exam than they hoped for.

This book consists of two main parts.

Part 1 talks about the first and most important question you have to ask yourself when it comes to studying. Why do you bother to study, anyway? Part 1 also demystifies the myths about getting good grades and sheds light on a two important words that make or break a student.

Part 2 is where the fun begins. Here, we reveal 10 most powerful study strategies that 'A' students use to get their 'A's. I've refined some of these strategies to make them more effective in today's context, and present them to you on a silver platter. Each of these 10 strategies will significantly change your grades for the better, only if you consistently adopt and apply them.

In order to get the most out of this book, there are 3 simple things you can do:

1. Be Open, Be Hungry

The well-known martial artist and actor, Bruce Lee, had a favorite story that he would tell to new students who wanted to learn martial arts from him, and I will be sharing this same story with you right now.

A man once went to visit a Zen master to learn the art of Zen. As the Zen teacher talked, the man frequently interrupted to express his own opinion. Finally the Zen teacher stopped talking and began to serve tea to the man. He poured the cup full, then kept pouring until the cup overflowed.

"Stop," said the man. "The cup is full, no more can be poured in."

"Like this cup you are full of your own opinions," replied the Zen teacher. "If you do not first empty your tea cup, how can you taste my cup of tea?"

Likewise, I want you to "empty your teacup" and be open and willing to try new ideas, new strategies and new forms of thinking. You must keep the energy and hunger to succeed going strong. Be relentless in spite of setbacks or challenges.

2. Apply whatever you've learned as soon as you can

Read and re-read each chapter again and again until you've completely understood it. Do all the activities in the book. Use a highlighter or pen to underscore key concepts, and write lots of notes of your ideas and thoughts in the blank spaces or in a separate notebook.

THE A LISTER

Most people read guides and self-development books just like they are reading a fiction storybook. Don't. If you really want to get results, do the exercises, the activities, and apply the strategies immediately when you start your next class or next revision for a test.

You'll probably find it tough to apply the strategies all of the time, and get disappointed or complain when the going gets tough. Remember, success doesn't happen in one day. What you're really doing is attempting to form new habits and ways of learning that are effective and efficient.

3. Share your successes and failures

The best way to make sure you constantly improve and grow is to share about your successes and your failures. Even with this book, I'm sure you will experience challenges and failures.

You can learn much more when you share your failures and share what you've learned from them. With each story, you make a declaration to the world that you will improve from them and grow stronger. You should also share your successes too. You shouldn't be afraid to share your wins with others, because you have worked hard for it. From these stories, you can identify the things that worked for you and the things that didn't work, and improve from there.

I'd also love to hear your stories after reading this book! If you have any success stories or "A-ha" moments after reading the book and applying the strategies in it, feel free to email them to **khinwai@thealisterbook.com**, with the subject "My Story".

PART 1:
WHY BOTHER STUDYING ANYWAY?

••••••••••••••••••••••••••••••••••••••

"The true purpose of education is to make the mind think!"

— Albert Einstein

Part 1: Why Bother Studying Anyway?

What is Your "Why"?

Before jumping in and learning about the different strategies to get amazing grades, the first and most important question you need to ask yourself is, "why do I want to improve my grades?"

When you figure out your "Why", the "how" becomes so much easier and attainable. This is because your "Why" triggers off an emotionally compelling reason to study well.

It's the same with life.

You will feel more motivated to do better and better at something that you have passion for, than with something you don't. Your "Why" is that burning fuel that will sustain you through periods when you feel like giving up.

A lot of my peers have been asking me this question, "How do I keep myself motivated to study?" And my answer will always be the same – find your "why".

How do you find your "Why"? Go inside your head and think about why getting good grades is so important to you.

Perhaps with good grades you will be able to get a scholarship or a study grant, which will offset a huge portion of your family's financial burdens.

Or maybe you've dreamt of travelling the world since you were a child, and getting good grades will open doors for you to get you one step closer to your dream.

Maybe you wanted good grades so that you can prove to your crush how intelligent you are, and increase your chances of going out with him or her.

Whatever it is, go deep within yourself to find the answer. Don't read the rest of this book till you have a very deep, emotional (and likely, personal) reason to get good grades, and are satisfied with it. Your "Why" must be so strong that it keeps you awake at night thinking about it.

Do It: Finding Your Why

Figuring out "why" you want to get good grades may seem simple, but it's not. You need a powerful reason that will drive you to do things and make you feel charged and energized.

Imagine that you are going to meet, face to face, with your favorite singer for lunch tomorrow. Just the two of you. How will that feel? Are you feeling so excited that you cannot sleep? Do you feel a strong rush of adrenalin through your body? That is the kind of feeling you will have once you've found your emotional "why".

There are so many reasons for being an "A" Lister. To help you out, I've listed a few here so that you can adapt from it to formulate your own personal "why":

- I want to get into University
- I want to relieve my family's financial burdens through getting awards and scholarships with good grades
- I want to prove my capabilities (Self-esteem)
- I want to attract a potential soulmate

THE A LISTER

- I want to be open to more possibilities in life
- I want to become "someone" in life
- I want to do good and contribute to the society using your knowledge
- I want to increase my knowledge of the world
- It is relevant to my future profession
- I want to get enjoyment from the sense of discovery / enlightenment
- I want to engage my mind intellectually
- I want to use my knowledge to help people in third-world countries by _____
- I want to gain a [benefit / credit / reward] in the future as a result of getting good grades
- I want to gain pleasure out of the act of learning itself

From "Delinquent" To Top Student

As a young boy, David Hoe quickly learned that his childhood was significantly different than that of other kids.

At the age of five, his parents had divorced. At age seven, his mother lost her sight due to a botched cataract operation and young David had to sell tissue paper and tidbits on the streets to make ends meet. When he was 12, his mother had a stroke and died.

His struggles continued when his poor PSLE results landed him in the Normal (Technical) stream and he mixed with bad company – where drinking and smoking were part of his lifestyle.

However, the turning point was when David met new friends and realized that he particularly enjoyed helping his peers in their schoolwork. It was at that time that he found his "why" – David decided that he wanted to be a teacher.

Of course, every worthwhile dream has its challenges. David soon found out that he had to have an O-Level certificate in order to teach, and there was close to zero chance for a Normal (Technical) student to do his O-Levels.

Nevertheless, David pushed himself and studied as hard as he could to realize his dream. He was even more resolute when he received support and care from his teachers and mentors. Eventually, he aced his exams and became the national top student in 2004.

Riding on this chance, David wrote in to the then Education Minister about his aspirations, with success. He was going to finally take his O's! With strong determination, he scored four distinctions and went on to Catholic Junior College.

Competing against his peers who came from good schools, David had to work extra hard to keep the pace. What kept him going was the desire to give hope to Normal-stream students. He mentions that "There are not too many Normal (Technical) success stories out there."

Alas, his hard work paid off and he now studies at one of the top local universities in Singapore, progressing toward his goal. Stating his bigger "Why", he says, "At the end of the day, it's about giving our best in whatever we are doing.

As a student, I give my best in my academic work. If doing my best means working through my corrections, I'll do it. As a son, I also do my best to honour my parents, and if it means saying "thank you" or taking the courage to apologise, I'll do it. Lastly, for me as a CCA leader, I do my best to lead with dignity.

When we give our very best, we leave no room for regrets."

One Important Thing Your School Probably Didn't Tell You About

As students, we're told that we needed to learn in a certain way, study certain fixed subjects, and throw up whatever we've memorized on standardized tests. And, if we follow that system religiously, we will most likely do fine.

However, many times when we follow the system, we get the exact opposite results. Students regurgitate material from their notes and textbooks and do a mass dump on tests without reading the questions, get big red crosses on their papers, and wonder why they didn't do well. Then, they start to blame themselves. They wonder if they're really not smart while others seem to do so well.

What's worse, the education system, being a results-only system, puts them into schools for the "less academically inclined" and that confirms the student's thought of being not so smart true.

What most students don't realize is we weren't taught the very important difference between studying and learning. Even if we were, it wasn't emphasized and adopted enough as compared to being taught algebra or the periodic table of elements.

According to the Oxford Dictionary, studying is "the devotion of time and attention to acquiring knowledge", or so the activity itself. While the meaning of learning is to "gain or acquire knowledge or skill by study, experience, or being taught", or the result of that activity which we call studying.

We can study till our faces turn blue, but whether we gain the skill or knowledge is a separate thing.

Take for example learning a language (e.g. French). We can take French classes and listen to countless French audiotapes for all we want, but if we don't actually go ahead and speak the language, make a few mistakes here and there, and simmer in the French culture, we will never learn French fluently enough to get past "Bonjour".

This is why people can say "I've studied for a whole damn day, but I don't seem to learn anything."

By understanding this key difference, you now know why most students study so hard and for such long hours, but forget everything as soon as they step into the examination hall.

Would You Like Some Fries With That?

To demonstrate why it's important to not just "study" but instead, learn, here is a humorous recount by Jay Leno.

THE A LISTER

I went into a McDonald's yesterday and said, "I'd like some fries." The girl at the counter said, "Would you like some fries with that?"

Forget rote memorization. Forget trying to squeeze every single fact and figure into your brain. Forget studying in a fixed learning style. Because today, school tests and examinations want you to apply whatever you've learnt into a scenario or a case study. They want you to reverse engineer a concept. They want your opinion on events close to home. They want counter-arguments and different perspectives from students. And, if you're flexible, resourceful, and creative enough to come up with fresh ideas and improvements, you will be ahead of the game.

So, the key takeaway I want you to understand here is DON'T STUDY, LEARN! You can be looking at a stack of notes for hours, yet nothing goes into your head. To LEARN is what we essentially want to do.

Two Traits of Highly Successful Students

All 'A' Listers have two things in common.

First is **FOCUS**. Did you ever notice that good students are always so focused at doing whatever they are doing? And this laser-focus is really what fuels their system to work so well. When you are focused, you give all your attention to learning, and that makes the best possible learning you can ever have.

I want you to think back at a moment in your life where you were really focused at doing something. It could be doing up a puzzle piece, baking a cake, reading a fantastic novel, etc... Did you find that time passes really quickly and you seemed to be enjoying yourself? You relished every moment filling up the puzzle pieces and decorating your cakes that it didn't seem like a chore.

And, as you're thinking about it right now, it is likely that you remember specific moments very clearly in your head. The picture that was on the puzzle. The design that you put on your cake.

Now the question, how are you going to put that same focus into your schoolwork and study materials? That's what we will be discussing more on in the second part.

The next quality great students all have is **PERSISTENCE**. They don't give up when the going gets tough. They don't give up seeing the mountains of homework they have. They don't give up when they have failed in a subject. In fact, they use the situation they are in and turn that into a learning experience in itself! How smart is that?

By mastering these two qualities, you already have the groundwork set. Being ahead of the competition is not difficult, you just need the mental grit and focus to get what you want.

Demystifying the Myths of Getting Good Grades

1. I can probably "wing it"

All 'A' Listers know one thing for sure – you can never get good grades by just "winging it". Sure, you may likely pass the test. But if you are serious in improving your results exponentially, you need to prepare and practice.

THE A LISTER

2. I need to be really intelligent to get 'A's

No you don't. What you need is practice and mastery. The only reason why intelligence is so often linked with getting good grades is because IQ was one of the only ways to measure student performance in the past. In today's terms, it has become obsolete. With the proper mindset and strategies in place, you can be well on your way to becoming an 'A' Lister.

3. I need to be a nerd to get good grades

A very big misconception a lot of students have is that they need to be a bookworm and stare at their textbooks all day long. If you were to observe your peers who have been acing all their exams and tests, they most likely have time for activities other than studying, like their sports, hobbies, jobs or time with family and friends.

What you need, however, is good time management, getting your priorities in order and being firm with yourself.

4. It's bad to be a grade grubber

What comes to mind when you think of an 'A' student? Do you see an under-socialized, selfish and competitive individual who always keeps to himself and stares at a book all the time? Or do you see a well-respected, well-learned individual who is outgoing, friendly and helpful to everyone around him?

It's easy to see high achievers in a negative light because of the attached stereotype. But I want you to challenge yourself to break that stereotype and associate yourself with the "new age of high achievers". Don't let that little voice control you, because there is nothing wrong with wanting to be the best that you can possibly be.

5. You learn and perform better in an absolutely quiet environment.

How many of us have heard this "advice" from our teachers or parents? According to a report published by Education Today in 1994, it stated that research has shown that many students think and remember best when studying with music and 20% of one elementary population scored significantly higher in reading in a noisy environment.

Before you start rushing to blast your home speaker systems with the latest hit from One Direction, there are some things to note.

Some students require absolute silence while learning, while others learn better with music on. So, it really depends. If you get distracted all the time and can't concentrate because you were humming along to the music every few seconds, you'd be better off WITHOUT music. We'll be covering this in the next part as well.

6. You learn best when seated upright at a desk or table.

The same research also concluded that students do better in informal environments. Sitting on a wooden or plastic chair in a classroom for prolonged periods of time causes stress on your spinal cord, and results in fatigue, discomfort and the constant need for change in sitting posture.

High school students from the US were studied, and they had shown great improvement in Math and English when taught and tested while seated on pillows, lounge chairs and carpets.

However, that doesn't mean that you can start studying while lying down on your bed! Do sit in an upright position anywhere you feel comfortable, but not too comfortable...

7. You learn best in well-lit areas and damage their eyes when they read and study in low light

It's a myth that students excel when studying in bright, white light. Most studies conducted had shown that white light (the ones used in dental offices) cause you to feel restless, fidgety and hyperactive.

Instead, low, dim lights help to calm you down and make you think more clearly. You only need enough light for comfortable reading, just make sure it's bright enough so that you don't squint to study your notes.

Teachers who permitted students to sit and work in low-light corners were surprised by their improved behaviour, attention and grades within six weeks. It was particularly good for underachievers!

Your Learning Style

Before we jump right into learning our strategies, you need to know what your learning style is so that you can adapt the strategies to match your learning style.

Not only will this help you to learn much better and faster, you will enjoy the process of learning much more, because you are learning in a way that you are most comfortable with.

There are 3 main types of learning styles – visual, auditory and kinesthetic.

Visual learners learn best by looking at information. For example, such learners can remember or understand things easier by looking at pictures of it, reading text off a book or watching a video about it.

Auditory learners learn best through listening to a voice explain the concept to them. Such learners may be found with earphones or headphones on most of the time listening to an audiobook. Sometimes, they may also learn through reading aloud to themselves or like to have music in the background playing while they study.

Kinesthetic (or Tactile) learners learn best through movement. They aren't able to sit still for a full hour studying, and will tend to fidget a lot. They may also play with things on the desk (such as twirling a pen or playing with a stress ball). Writing stuff down allows them to understand a concept much better. They also prefer to do practical-based rather than theory-based work, as they get to handle objects and learn at the same time.

After reading the three types of learning styles, which one do you feel you lean more towards to or use more of?

If you still haven't got a clue, take a short quiz at this website to figure out your learning style: **http://www.educationplanner.org/students/self-assessments/learning-styles-quiz.shtml**

Among the three learning styles, the visual learner learns the fastest and the easiest. This is because our eyes allow a lot of information to flow through at once, while the ears and other sensory functions of the body process information in chunks.

However, don't be discouraged if you're not much of a visual learner. Visual learning can be improved. It's more important that you don't label yourself as purely a visual learner or purely an auditory learner. The most effective learning takes place when all modes of learning are used in conjunction with each other.

PART 2:
Revealing 10 Powerful Study Strategies in Every 'A' Listers' Arsenal

....

"In real life, strategy is actually very straightforward. You pick a general direction and implement like hell"

— Jack Welch

THE A LISTER

Part 2: Revealing 10 Powerful Study Strategies in Every 'A' Listers' Arsenal

I've picked out 10 of the most powerful study techniques that absolutely any student can apply to supercharge their grades.

Some of these strategies have been used by top memory masters in the world, and can be applied in many, if not all, of the subjects or modules that you are currently learning.

I've personally applied all of the strategies you're about to learn in my own student's journey, and am a living testament of how effective these strategies were for me, and how they can also be for you.

THE **A LISTER**

STRATEGY #1

The Key is In the Keywords

"A very little key will open a very heavy door"

- Charles Dickens,
Author of *Hunted Down*

Keywords are words every examiner will look out for so that they can award you marks. They are considered so important that without them, you could virtually score zero even if you've written a huge chunk of text.

Remember, the goals is to be concise and focused with your answer. And keywords do just that without going into too much detail in your answers. Keywords save you time, brain juice and writing space. So be sure to use it.

Keywords are basically the most important words in a sentence or a paragraph. These are the ones you should be paying attention to. The rest of the words are called filler words. Here's an example:

[**What is an electrical conductor?** An electrical conductor is a substance that **permits electrons** to **flow through** it **easily**. Most metals are good conductors.]

The topic at hand is "what is an electrical conductor". As you can see, we can immediately break down the definition of an electrical conductor from 19 words to just 5 keywords – "permit electrons flow through easily". There is no keyword for the second sentence as it elaborates on the first sentence by giving us an example.

Identifying keywords accurately is a skill that you can only acquire by observing and practicing often. Find out which words gives a sentence its full meaning.

Find out what are the key ideas that the book wants you to take away.

One way to do this is firstly by skimming over the chapter that you are trying to understand. Read it like how you would read your favourite magazine or comic book.

Then, look at what are the key ideas to be taken away from the book. Most textbooks and module notes would have a "chapter outline" section or "chapter summary" at the beginning or the end of the chapter.

Finally, once you know what to look out for, use a highlighter and highlight all the relevant keywords.

Another way to identify keywords is to eliminate the filler words. Filler words are words like "the", "a", "very" and "usually".

Essentially, what you are doing when you are identifying keywords is you are summarizing the whole sentence or paragraph into a few words, while retaining the overall meaning of the original text.

THE A LISTER

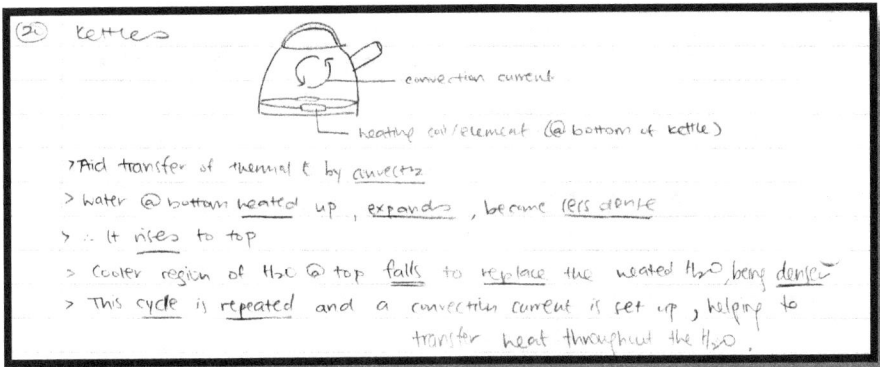

An example of how keywords are being used

Using Keywords in Note-Taking

Do you find yourself scribbling furiously away during lectures because of all that information you're trying to take down? Stop, and take a look to the "A" Listers. They seem to be super calm and I bet you, they are one of the fastest students to ever finish taking down notes in class.

The efficient note-taker's writing case would always consist of these few things – a highlighter (or two) and a pen. No glitter markers and no fancy pencils.

The 'A' listers wouldn't be furiously writing away at every word the lecturer says. They would pay very close attention to the words being said, identify the keywords or key points, and write them out or highlight them if they're already in the textbook or module notes.

HO KHINWAI

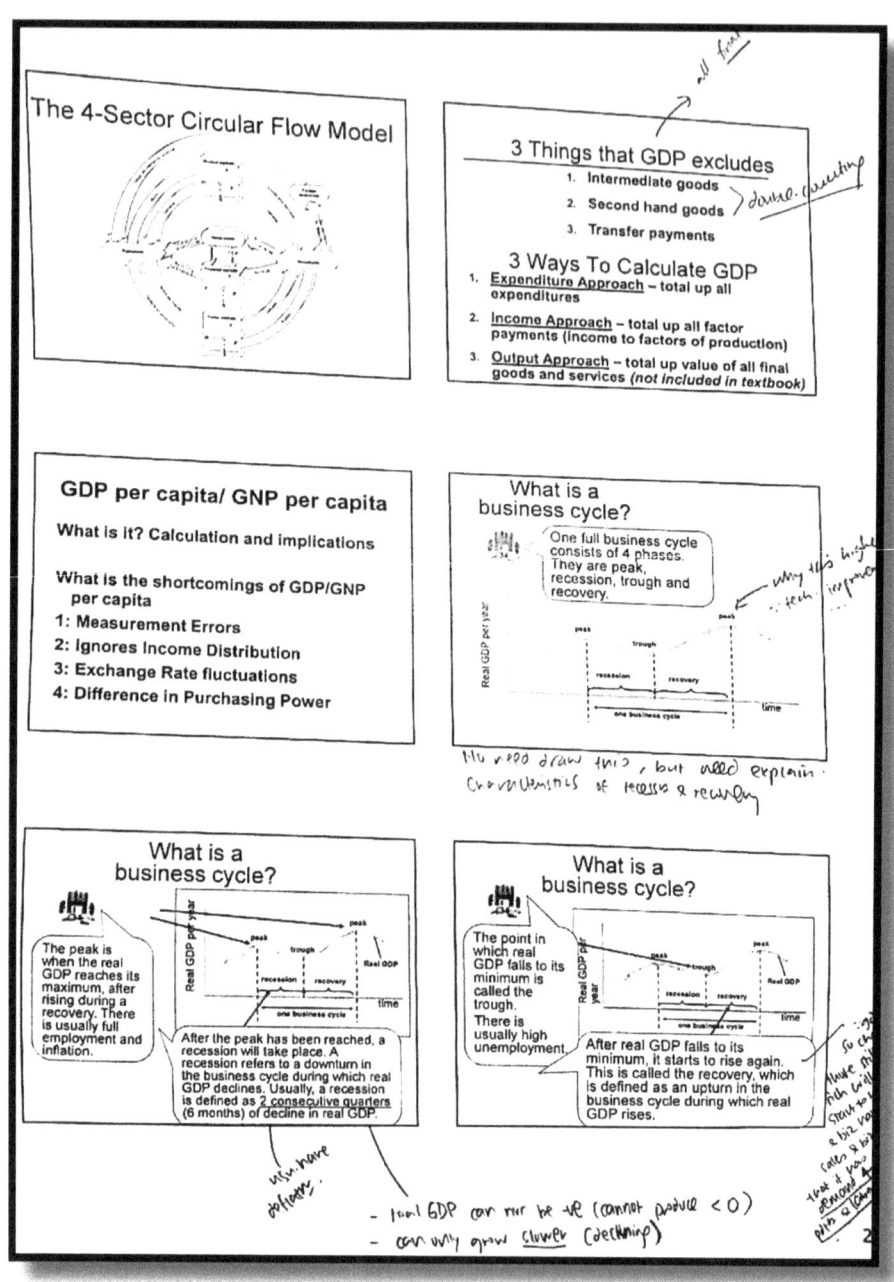

A page from my module notes. Notice that I've annotated a few of the slides with important information from the lecture

THE A LISTER

The other secret to taking super-quick notes like the pros is to use abbreviations and symbols.

Abbreviations are shortened words that can be existing or made up. You are probably already using some of them when you text your friends on WhatsApp. Some examples are "you" becomes "u", "to" becomes "2", "because" becomes "coz" or "bcoz".

I also use certain Greek symbols or other symbols that connote a certain word or meaning, just so that I save that small amount of time used to write a word.

Don't belittle the insignificance of the amount of time saved. When added up, it's a great deal! What's more, every second counts in note taking...

Just to give you a visual idea of what they are and how to use them, here is a table of some of the abbreviations and symbols I've used for my note taking.

ABBREVIATIONS		SYMBOLS	
LONG FORM	SHORT FORM	LONG FORM	SHORT FORM
I don't know	Idk	Therefore	∴
opportunity	Oppn	Because	∵
house	Hse	Directly related / proportional	∝
because	Coz / bcoz	Not transferrable	T̶r̶s̶f̶
book	Bk	and	&
relationship	rlshp	at	@
calculator	calc	[same words as above]	"

More abbreviations and symbols can be found by going to the links below*:

http://goo.gl/U0Dedd

http://goo.gl/lxj8l1

*resources not owned by me

THE A LISTER

> WHAT CAUSES EXCH.RATE TO △
> (supply & demand factors)

"Exchange rate" becomes "Exch. Rate" and the triangle represents "change".

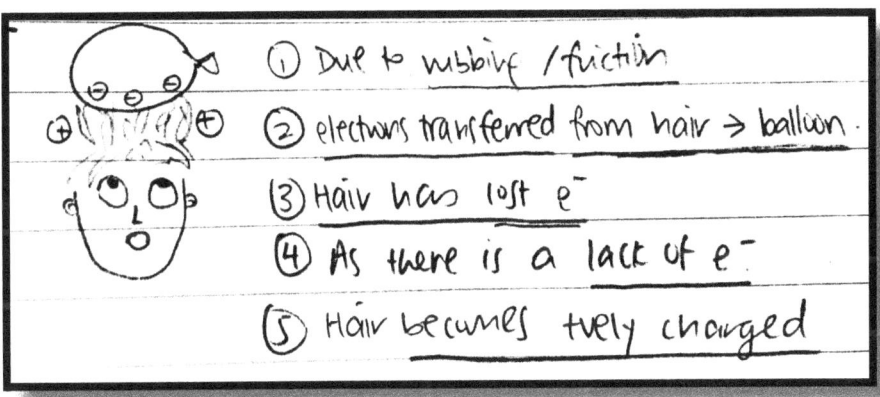

The arrow in Step 2 represents "to", "e-" in Step 3 and Step 4 represents electrons, and "+vely" in Step 5 means "positively".

There are a thousand and one symbols and abbreviations that you can choose to use. However, the more important thing is that you recognize what you're writing down, and it's easy for you to decipher it back to yourself.

It might be a little weird and uncomfortable to use when you're first starting out, but once you are familiar with it, you'll be taking notes like a pro.

A tip: If you're using separate sheets of paper to take your notes, don't spend too much time designing and making them look nice.

Most notes never get read and are chucked to a corner. And, you run the risk of misplacing or losing them. So, make sure you staple them to the textbook once you're done, so that you won't lose them and are able to reference back to the main text in the future.

THE A LISTER

Activity: Fishing 4 Keywords

You've now learnt two quick tips in this Strategy – How to find keywords and abbreviating your notes. Now it's your turn to put them to use:

1. Take out a textbook or any of your class notes and flip open to any chapter that you've already studied. With a highlighter or a pen, go through the chapter and highlight or circle any keywords that may be important.

When in doubt, ask yourself, "If I could set the test for this chapter, what would I include in the test?"

2. Before your next class, get familiar with one or two abbreviations that you would like to incorporate in your note-taking.

2 Abbreviations I'd Like To Use...

1) _____

2) _____

In your next class, be sure to use them whenever your lecturer is giving you additional information that isn't found in your textbook or class notes!

Practice using them until you no longer have to consciously replace the full word with the abbreviation.

THE A LISTER

STRATEGY #2

The Memory Quadrant

"If you study to remember, you will forget. But if you study to understand, you will remember"

- Unknown

One of the biggest obstacles that students face in their studies is not being able to remember what they have learned when they sit for their exams.

Most students enter the exam hall in a confused state of mind, only remembering bits and pieces of information they've studied from the day before!

What if I told you that you can stop being envious of "those top students who are born with a great memory" and be in the big league of 'A' Listers where, in turn, your peers envy you for your memory prowess?

What if as a direct result of using just 4 simple memory techniques, you are now able to supercharge your memory power so you can score those 'A's in exams and tests?

This is why I've designed **The Memory Quadrant**. It is a toolbox of four great memory techniques that will enable you to remember and recall information faster and easier.

The Memory Quadrant™

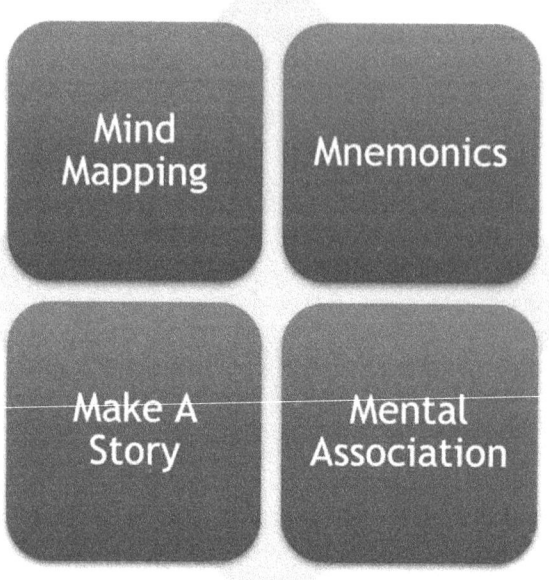

These tools are used by the top memory champs in the world to remember information quickly and accurately. You, too, can now tap on these powerful tools to supercharge your memory!

You may be familiar with some of the techniques in this toolbox, but you may not be using them to your fullest advantage.

1. Mind Mapping

You probably might've come across the idea of mind maps. Have you used them? How did you feel about them?

Personally, when I first started to use mind maps, I didn't like it at all. I like my information to be neat and structured.

THE A LISTER

So, I didn't find the idea of stems and leaves branching out in different directions very helpful.

After fiddling with it for a bit, I realized if I moved the main topic to the top, and branch my sub-items out in a hierarchical fashion, I now had a clean and organized mind map that I was comfortable learning from.

I really enjoyed making mind maps (in my style) from then on, because I could fit all the keywords and key details neatly into one single sheet of paper and just study using that piece of paper!

All the information had been neatly compressed, and I could see how each point links back to the main topic. My mind maps aren't that colorful or illustrative as you can see, but they work for me.

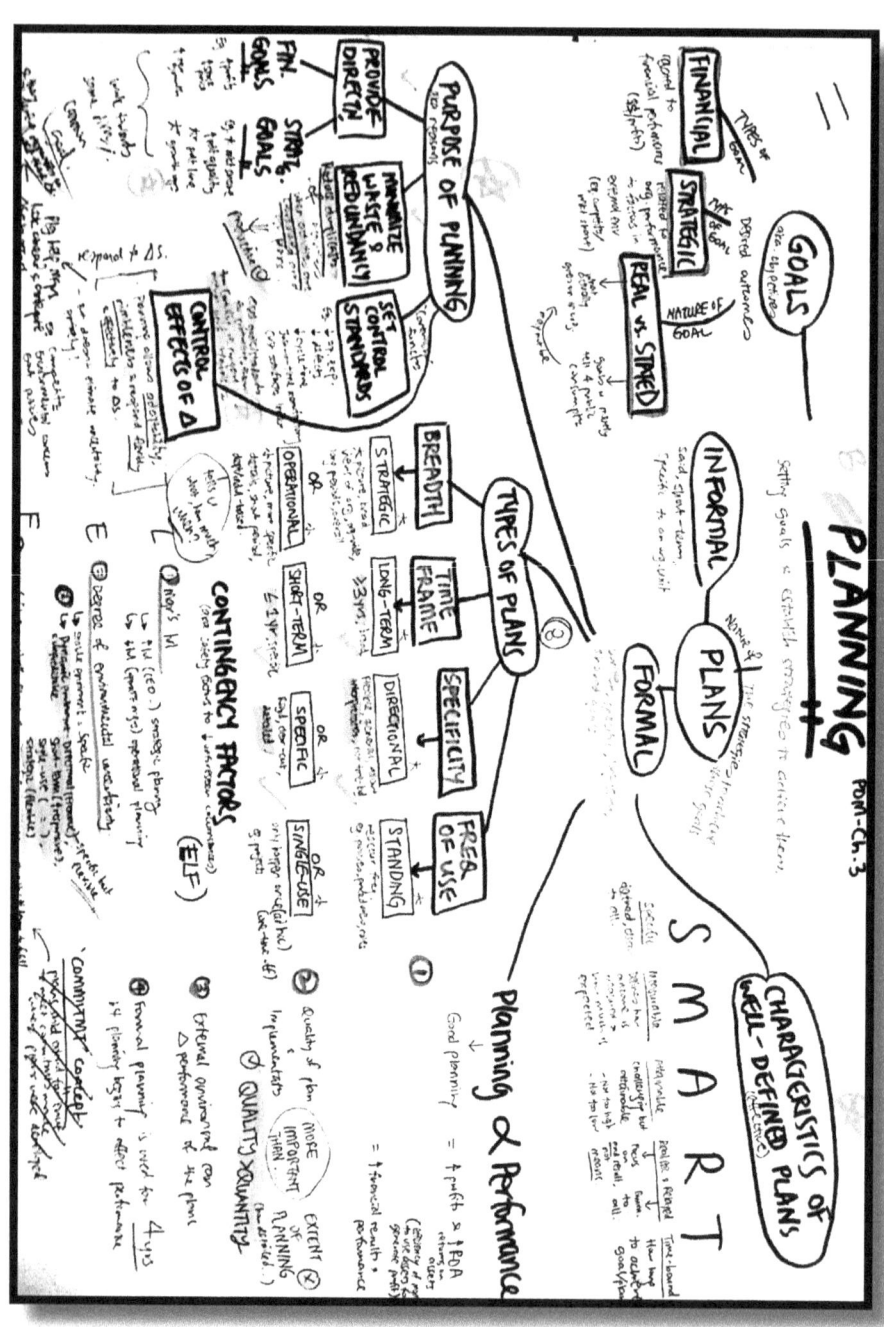

My mind map. Notice where the topic title is compared with the next one.

THE A LISTER

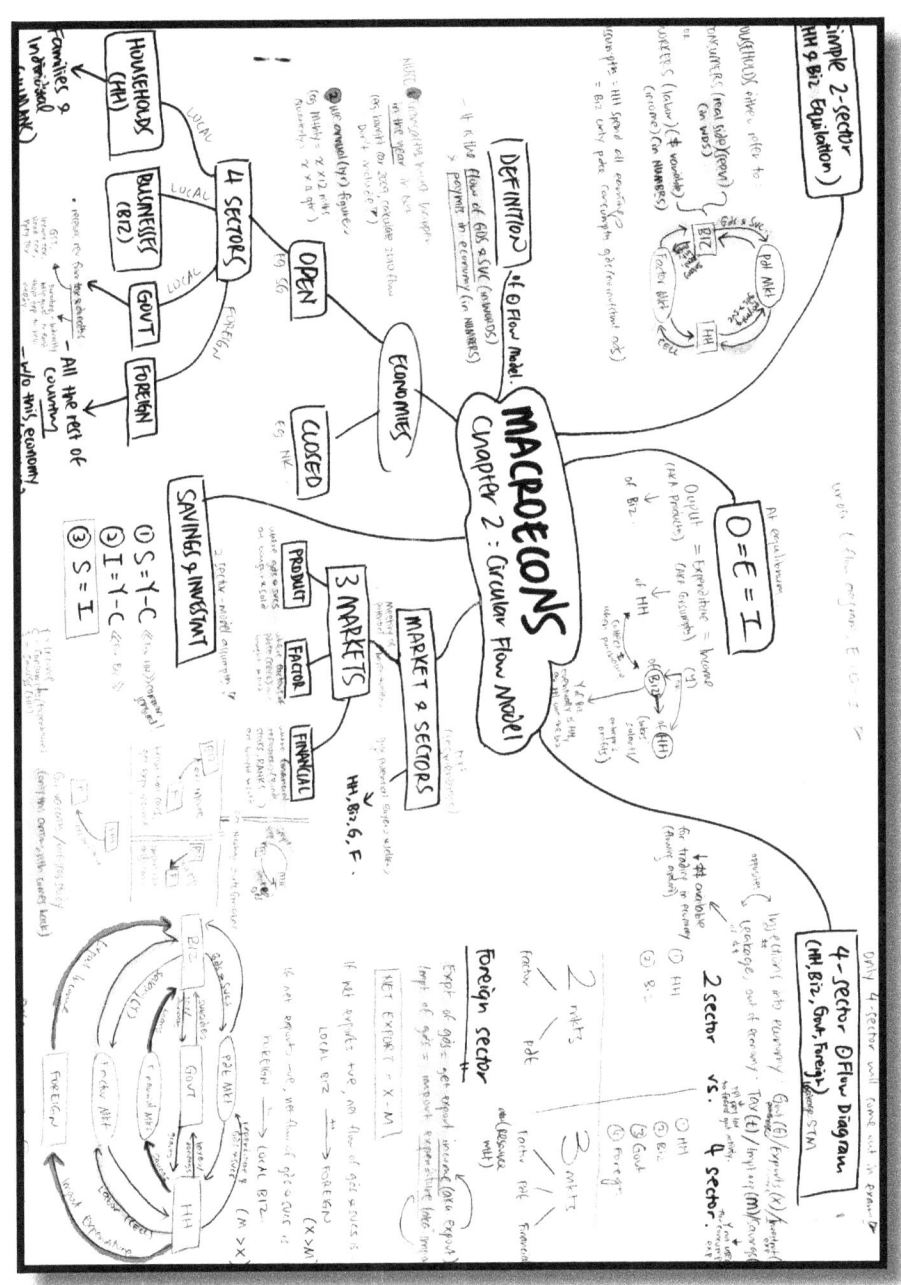

A traditional mind map created with the central topic branching out.

During test or exam periods, I'd have only just a few sheets of paper for my revision, and I just study from those mind maps I've created.

In less than half an hour, I could complete my whole revision for the entire subject and go back to revising it for another time. Just before the exam, I would take out a folder of all my mind maps, neatly filed and stapled, and refresh my mind for one last time before I step into the exam hall. No more furiously flipping through pages, getting all flustered just because you forgot which page the explanation for a convection current is on.

So, if you haven't already used mind maps because there are "a lot of rules to follow" or you "keep having to change marker colors" or "they're confusing", play around with how your mind maps are structured and figure out how best you can use them for accelerated learning.

Remember, such tools and strategies are there to serve you in your learning, not limit you. Take the standard rules for doing up a mind map as a guideline and nothing more. It's much more important you create your own style to fit your learning needs.

2. Mnemonics

Mnemonics are also a very common memory technique you might've come across. They are any tool that helps you to remember information otherwise difficult to recall. Mnemonics are used heavily by memory masters.

In fact, a scientist studied the top eight contenders in the "World Memory Championships" and revealed that their brains were no different than that of the brains of normal, average people. On the whole, they weren't smarter than others as well. Their supernormal memory was solely because

THE A LISTER

they had mastered the skill of using mnemonics.

There are many types of mnemonics. In this book, I'm going to show you a few types of mnemonics that you can immediately use in your studies.

Acronyms

Acronyms take the first letter of a list of words or items and string them together to form a memorable word or phrase. One example you probably know are the 7 colors of the rainbow, or ROY G BIV – Red, Orange, Yellow, Green, Blue, Indigo, and Violet.

Acronyms are easy to remember and useful if you need to remember a list of items.

You can create your own acronyms whenever you need to memorize lists of words. For example,

The four magnetic materials are

- Iron
- Steel
- Cobalt
- Nickel

I can either call them NICS or I can call them Nicofes (Nickel, Cobalt, Iron (Fe), Steel). For me, I found that Nicofes stuck in my head a bit more, so I went with that.

Try different combinations and pick the one that sticks in your head the most.

You can also reverse engineer acronyms. Instead of creating a new word, you use the letters to make a phrase or a sentence.

These are called acrostics.

One common example you are sure to come across if you're a beginner musician is the phrase Every Good Boy Does Fine, or EGBDF, the notes on the lines of a treble clef.

Personally, I rely a lot on acronyms. Especially for definitions, if there are important keywords within it.

However, depending on what you are trying to remember, sometimes it's difficult to create an acronym for your list of things. In that case, the next best way is to create an acrostic, or to use some other memory tool to remember it.

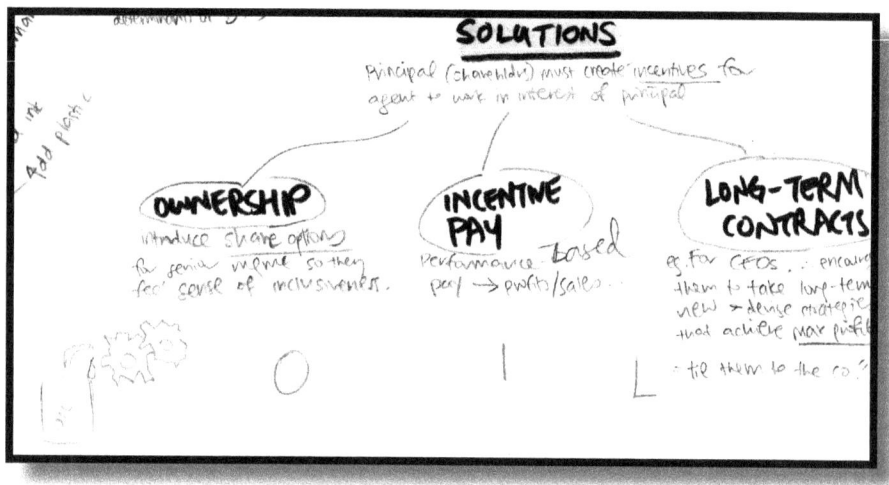

Here, I used the first letter of each keyword to form an acronym "OIL"

Models

Model mnemonics help you remember hierarchical structures, levels or relationships by visually presenting you with a diagram. Such diagrams may include pyramids, cycles, matrices, process flows, quadrants, or hierarchy charts.

THE A LISTER

In fact, the Memory Quadrant itself is a model mnemonic I designed specifically to help you remember the 4 memory techniques!

Also, did you notice that all the items in the Memory Quadrant start with the same letter 'M'? I combined both acronyms and the model, so that you can still remember the 4 memory tools long after you've closed this book.

Models are meant to be simple frameworks to help you structure and organize information in a way that is easy to recall. Therefore, there should be no complicated diagrams, arrows pointing to every direction or a whole paragraph of words littering the model. Essentially, it should be kept clean and anyone who looks at it should be able to understand it immediately.

Models are all around you. Look at Maslow's Hierarchy of Needs. Look at the 4 Ps of Marketing. Look at the Water Cycle. And look at the Food Pyramid. These are all models mapped out to make complicated processes easy to understand and digest.

Use them whenever you want to remember complicated processes, systems, structures and relationships.

Music and Rhymes

Quick, what's the chorus to Miley Cyrus's 'Wrecking Ball'?

You probably remember the lyrics to it, don't you? In fact, if I asked you to write out the entire chorus of the song 'Wrecking Ball', you could most likely do it in less than five minutes, and with all the correct words in order!

Songs are hard to forget, especially if they're super catchy and have an awesome rhythm to them. Understanding that, you can use the same method to your studies, too!

You might wish to create a short song or jingle if you have complex details you need to remember.

In fact, that's probably how you learned the alphabets when you were a child, by singing the ABC song over and over again. If you don't feel you have the time or talent to create a song, go on **www.youtube.com** and search for your topic that you need to remember and add the word "song" at the end. For common topics, most likely someone has already created a song for it.

I remembered back when I was in Secondary School, we had to learn the quadratic formula. To help us memorize the formula, our teacher played us the "quadratic formula song" and it got stuck in my head ever since.

Pilots in training use rhymes to help them remember if air pressure or temperature falls, their aircraft will go lower in altitude than what is indicated on the aircraft's dashboard, and vice versa.

High to low, look out below. Low to high, clear blue sky.

You can also create a short song, a poem or a rhyme whenever you feel that the topic or subject is too dull and you can't seem to remember anything.

THE A LISTER

3. Make A Story / Scene

Another powerful tool to remember information and details is to make a story or a scene out of the keywords. This is a great tool to use if you need to remember a number of keywords in sequence, but may not seem related.

For visual learners, this memory strategy works like a charm. For auditory learners, repeat the story to yourself over and over again. For kinesthetic learners, immerse yourself in the story and go through the motion of the story with props and gestures.

For example, we want to memorize the items on the electromagnetic spectrum, starting from Radio waves, Microwaves, Infrared, Visible, Ultraviolet, X-rays and Gamma Ray. Let's try spinning a story to help us remember the 7 items.

"A radio (radio waves) had been turned on and a Justin Bieber song was playing. A grizzly bear took the radio set and threw it into the microwave oven (microwave) and watched as it turned red hot (infrared) and heated up. Boom! The microwave caused a loud explosion, alerting hunters. Terrified, the bear chanted an invisibility (visible) spell, but it turned him into an ultra-sized (ultraviolet) bear instead! Now, the hunters, who were the X-men (X-ray) had found the bear and cornered him. Just then, his strong and powerful grandma bear (Gamma ray) shot them all down with a machine gun."

Now, close your eyes and try to envision the story coming alive using your imagination.

Done? Did you recall the story in vivid detail? Were you able to see the seven keywords through the whole story even though you've only just read this story once?

Stories are powerful magnets to the mind. If I asked you to remember the story of the three little pigs, little red riding hood or Cinderella, you'd probably be able to list down all the important scenes in the story by perfect sequence. Even though the last time you heard that story was 5 or 10 years ago!

To use stories effectively, it needs to be vivid and interesting. In Three Little Pigs, you could "see" how menacing and cunning the wolf was, and how the pigs worked hard to build a house to stop the wolf from getting to them. In my example story, you saw how the grizzly bear tried to become invisible, but evolved into an "ultra-bear" and was found by the X-men.

Another way to make stories stick better is to make it as weird and crazy as you can! The sillier the story, the better. Why? Our brains tend to filter out things that we already have experienced before, and deem them as redundant. This process is called Sensory Gating, in technical terms.

THE A LISTER

To get your brain to pay attention, it has to seem unusual or outstanding. This is why in my story, you'll see a how grandma bear appeared to save the day with her machine gun.

After you've remembered many stories for your particular subject, you'll be able to quickly whip out a story and its key points whenever you need it, be it in exams or tests.

4. Mental Association

Mental association is another memory technique by which you link the object you want to remember to an image. To "associate" is to create a connection, and scientific studies have shown that the best way to create this connection is through visual images.

So, if you can associate information you want to remember with familiar images you can easily visualize, the information will stick much more easily in your head.

Mental Association techniques are sometimes called memory pegs, memory palaces or anchors. This technique is highly learnable and usable, and is one of the best techniques to remember anything, from facts to names to dates to even foreign words.

How association works is simple. First, we break up the syllables of the word we want to remember. Then, we associate the sound of each syllable to a familiar object or action. Lastly, we link all the objects and actions to form a single image which can be easily recalled.

For instance, if we want to remember that "allegro" in music theory means "fast", we first break "allegro" into its syllables, which are "alle" and "gro". Then, now I try to associate the sounds with a familiar picture. For me, alle sounds like Allez in French, which means "go" and with "gro"

I also think of the word "go". So, two "go"s means go very quickly, like someone cheering me on in a race "Go! Go! Go!".

However, you might not associate with the same image as me. You might associate the whole word with "illegal" and conjure up the image of robbers quickly running away from the police, and the chase is being associated with being "fast".

How sticky the image is will depend on how specific and vivid your image is. Instead of just visualizing cops chasing robbers, you can bump the imagery up and see police lights flashing everywhere in the dark night and the sounds of the police sirens filling your ears.

It looks like there are many things going on at the same time, but when you keep associating that image with the word you want to remember, when you need to recall what the word means, the image immediately pops up in your mind as a still in a split second, losing no time for you to recall the information.

It Looks Like...

Another way of remembering information is to associate them with what the words or characters look like.

For example, I used to have much trouble differentiating between "horizontal" and "vertical". What I did to differentiate the two is to take the "v" in vertical and imagine it as an arrow being shot down from above, because "v" looks like the tip of an arrow that is pointing down. Then, horizontal would naturally be the other direction.

Another popular way is to see that the letter "V" looks like the letter "U", which is then associated with the word, Upright.

Get the idea?

THE A LISTER

Mental association is a great tool to use to remember complicated words like technical terms and jargon. These things are what actors, top students and memory masters use to recall information, and it works.

Once you've experimented with it for a bit, you'll find that it's a lot of fun to learn in this way, and your friends and teachers will be surprised how much your memory has seemed to improve!

Activity: The Memory Master

Congratulations! You've now learnt four powerful memory techniques in this Strategy – Mindmaps, Mnemonics, Making a Story and Mental Association. Now it's your turn to put them to use:

1. Refer back to the Exercise in Strategy #1, 'Fishing for Keywords' and pull out the chapter where you have your keywords circled and highlighted out.

Pull out a blank piece of A4-sized paper, a pen or pencil, some coloured markers (those thin felt-tip ones) and a few highlighters.

In your own style and way that you feel most comfortable with, start drawing up your mindmap. If anytime you feel that your mindmap won't work for you because it's too messy, confusing or whatever, stop and restart on a new sheet of paper and try out another style of drawing it. Remember, there are no hard and fast rules about this, you just have be comfortable with the process and confident with your "masterpiece".

2. When you are doing up your mindmap, you will most likely encounter parts where you need to remember a list of keywords or "sub-sub points" as I like to call them.

Wherever possible, implement the use of acronyms, abbreviations, models, rhymes, pictorial associations and story-telling into the mindmap.

THE A LISTER

STRATEGY #3
Manage This, And You Can Manage Anything

"The bad news is time flies. The good news is you're the pilot"

- Michael Altshuler,
Author & Motivational Speaker

We all only have 24 hours in a day. Why, then, are some students able to achieve a lot (CCAs, studies, hobbies, spending time with family and friends, playing games) while others seem to barely get enough time?

The secret is in the way people manage their time. Yeah, yeah, time management is such a passé topic, but guess what, it's one of the most essential things you need to master because everything in your life depends on time.

Imagine if you have a dinner appointment with your crush, and for some reason, you were late because you missed the bus, your keys got misplaced, you spilled your Starbucks Frappuccino all over your shirt and had to get new clothes. Eventually, your date thinks she's been stood up and there goes your chance. You don't want that happening to you, do you?

All of us know we need to manage our time better, but how? One of the greatest devils that messes up our daily schedule or our to-do list is procrastination.

Everyone suffers from procrastination. Even I have fallen prey to procrastination many, many, many times. Stopping procrastination is not very hard actually. We just need to make decisions on what is important at this moment (our priorities) and then getting it done immediately. This will put you in the fast lane towards academic success.

How to crush procrastination?

Either do it or don't.

It takes only a split second for you to decide whether to do something or not, and if you decide you are going to do it, make an effort to get it done now.

Stop whatever you are doing and do the task that you wanted to push away till later. It may feel dreadful and tough, but that's the only quick way you are going to get things done.

No use committing the task to a diary or putting it in your to-do list. Research shows that almost half of to-do items never get completed!

If you don't want to do it, but have to, here are some tips for you.

Find a motivation to do it. When you have a motivation to do something, you will naturally get around doing it. This is why having a purpose (you have identified that in Part 1) is so important.

It takes self-discipline and great motivation to stop procrastination. However once you break through this barrier, your life will start to transform. Amazing things will start to happen in both your studies and your personal life. You will feel more confident and gain a greater sense of self-control.

Beating procrastination is one thing, but being efficient and effective in how you study is another. In the same period of time, two students can have different productive levels and outputs.

'A' students know this, and this is why they seem to do so much in such a seemingly short time. And it is this reason that I want to share with you a few tips to maximize your productivity when you're studying.

How to Be More Productive?

Being able to do little yet reap a lot is every student's ideal study formula. Though not always possible there are some interesting ways this can be achieved to some level of satisfaction for all.

Productivity is generally measured by the resulting outcome produced and if this outcome is acceptable then the productivity percentage is deemed acceptable too, therefore understanding the elements that are required are where the answer lies.

1. Setting daily targets with the main goal always in focus helps to keeping objectives on track and in focus always. It also prevents you from wasting time on activities that won't positively contribute to the goal. We'll discuss goals in the next strategy.

2. Identifying your own "magic time" for being productive is also another "tool" to take advantage of. Having the energy to be productive throughout the day is not only unlikely it is also improbable; therefore there is a need to capitalize on the productivity time frame and get as much done within this frame as possible.

Identifying your "magic time" to study requires trial-and-error. Try studying in the early in the morning (before school), afternoon (after school) and at night, and notice which times you felt the most tired and at which times you felt most alert and ready to go.

After you have figured out your peak times, the next thing is to protect that time from any distractions and interruptions.

Should I Multitask?

It seems to be an obsession, especially in this day and age where we have technology and Internet connection, that multitasking seems like a good thing.

People generally think that top students and high achievers are really great multitaskers who seem to appear super busy and super flustered every day. Apparently, multitaskers seem to be celebrated not only in school, but in work life, where you think of a businessman who is taking a phone call, while typing away at his laptop at the same time.

For students, you might already be embracing the idea of multitasking by watching your favourite Korean drama on YouTube, texting your best friend and studying all at the same time.

The truth is, by multitasking, you're actually being less productive in your studies and might end up having to take MORE TIME to re-read your material to understand what the heck it is trying to say.

Research has shown that we aren't made to multitask, especially on things that require brainpower like learning. Our short term memory is only able to store between 5 and 9 things at a go.

THE A LISTER

At any one second, your brain receives a lot of external information and stimuli. When you multitask, you limit the capacity for your brain to store the necessary studied material, because some of the brain's resources are being used to process your other activities, like responding to your friends' text message or understanding what's going on in the drama.

To be 100% productive and receptive to what you're trying to learn, you need to be absolutely focused. Instead of improving your multitasking skills, improve your focus skills. Learn how to prioritize what's important and be efficient at doing one thing at a time. If you're constantly jumping from one activity to the other, you're wasting time doing everything but end up achieving very little on each task.

Also, when you are focused on doing one thing at a time, you find that the work you do is of a much better quality, and whatever you are trying to memorize or learn gets stuck in your head much easier and much longer.

HO KHINWAI

Activity: The Hocus-Focus

Today, as you're reading this, decide on one thing that you want to accomplish by the end of the day. Just ONE thing. Not two, not three, not four.

It could be as simple as not watching TV for the entire day. Or, drinking 8 glasses of water today. Or, not sleeping in class today. Whatever. Just decide on one and write it in the box below:

After you've decided, make that goal your priority for the day.

Focus on channelling all your energies into completing that task. Constantly remind yourself throughout the day. Repeat it to yourself if you wish, or set up reminders on your smartphone.

At the end of the day, check back and see if you have completed the goal. If you have, great job! Give yourself a pat on the back for staying focused. If you have not, ask yourself what was the main reason that stopped you from completing

THE A LISTER

my task today?

Don't feel bad about it, instead, this is an opportunity to gain an insight into your behaviours and find the root of your procrastination!

To help you out, here are a few questions to reflect on. Write your answers (brutally and shamelessly) in the blank spaces below.

1. What do you think was the main cause for not completing the task today? (If you have many answers, just pick the strongest one you felt had most impact in screwing up your plans)

_____

2. If you had to complete this same task again the next day, how would you avoid the barrier in Question 1?

_____

_____

_____

THE A LISTER

STRATEGY #4

Having A Game Plan

"Whenever you want to achieve something, keep your eyes open, concentrate and make sure you know exactly what it is you want. No one can hit their target with their eyes closed"

— Paulo Coelho,
Author of 'The Alchemist'

"Goaaaaaaaallllll!"

If you've ever seen or played football (or any kind of competitive sport) before, you would know that there will certainly be some kind of game plan laid out before each match.

You must've certainly seen this scene on television before: You're in the guys' locker room. You and your teammates are gathered in a crowd, sweaty and serious. And in front of you is your coach.

He says, "This is your last match. The strongest player in the opponent team is down. Now, here's what you got to do…"

As coach begins drawing on the board, the chalk screeches with each definite stroke, revealing the ultimate game plan to win the final match.

Why is it that the coach bothers to spend that precious 10 – 20 minutes strategizing and laying down a game plan, instead of letting the team rest?

Because a game plan tells you exactly your role as a player, what you're expected to do in that match, and the approach you are going to use to successfully get the ball into the goalpost. There is no confusion. Just a well-thought out plan for winning.

A study goal is just like a game plan, except that you score marks instead of goals.

Most students, and that includes many of my friends, don't have study game plans. That's why their grades keep fluctuating, and they are unable to consistently get better and better at their game!

A pirate needs a map to locate the hidden treasure chest. Without it, he may chance upon some gold nuggets searching for it, but will never be able to find the big loot.

So, do you have your "map" with you?

Don't worry if you don't, because in this chapter, you'll discover how to easily devise your own study game plan even if you have no clue how to do it.

THE A LISTER

The Top 3 Reasons Why Most Students Don't Set Goals

Most students hate setting study goals or study game plans. We're never really taught how to do it the right way, and this causes some confusion and frustration for most students. In the end, the goals they've set are forgotten, or don't get done at all. Here are the top 3 reasons that students will usually say about goal setting.

1. "I Don't Know How To?"

When was the last time you had set a goal? No, I'm not talking about New Years' Resolutions. When was the last time you had actually sat down and made a game plan of achieving a certain dream?

Too long ago to remember?

Well the thing is, most of us were taught in school to just imagine in our minds about our dreams and goals and how we wanted to achieve them. We were never really taught to sit down and write it out on a piece of paper our goal and the steps needed to achieve them.

As we got older, we were more intrigued by games and smartphones that goal setting was just another thing to put off till tomorrow.

2. "I've tried. It doesn't work!"

To that question, I ask, "Have you figured out why it did not work for you?"

Most people see goal setting as a one-time kind of thing. If it don't work, it don't work. In truth, goals are a constant thing you need to maintain and keep track of. You may need to modify it a little, extend the timeframe just a bit or rework the entire plan during the process.

In a later segment, I'll reveal one stunning secret of goal setting that ALL successful people know about, and this will be part of your own game plan you would use to get them "A"s.

3. "Too Tedious and Slow to See Results."

Let me go off-topic here for a while and make a wild guess that your mobile phone or tablet device is just an arm's length away from you.

Was I right?

It doesn't matter. The point I'm trying to make is that we all are living in a high-speed, interconnected and rapid-changing society today.

The first iPhone was out just less than a decade ago, and now look, we're at the iPhone 6 now. Imagine that! Six iPhone improvements in less than a decade! With the internet today, you could send an email and buy that bag you've always wanted almost instantly.

We want to do something now and see results fast. We have microwavable one-minute meals, instant noodles, diet coke, fast food and fast internet. We can't stand Internet Explorer when we now have Google Chrome, and we get frustrated when there's a long queue at the counter. We're all living in an instant gratification society, if you haven't got the message already!

What ever happened to delayed gratification?

Goals are just like potted plants. They need time to grow and sprout. You will only achieve "A"s if you are patient and committed to your goals. This is true for every dream,

THE A LISTER

aspiration, or goal that you have – be it getting "A"s, being wealthy, or finding love.

The Chinese Bamboo Tree

The Bamboo tree is one of the most versatile and strongest trees in the world. It can withstand extreme winds and weather storms.

What you may not know is that the bamboo tree doesn't grow like a typical tree. Unlike trees which grow steadily over the years, there is no growth in the first four years. No signs of sprouting at all, even when the seeds are carefully watered and fertilized each day.

In the fifth year, that Chinese bamboo tree seed finally sprouts and the bamboo tree grows up to eighty feet in just a few weeks! It's almost as if you could see it growing right before your eyes!

All success, regardless academic or not, works in a similar way. You need faith, perseverance and the ability to "wait it out".

The bamboo seeds had to be watered and fertilized every day without fail. If the farmers were to miss a day of tending, the bamboo will die.

Successful 'A' Listers know that there are no "overnight successes". Behind all the wins are hard work, persistence and an unwavering faith to succeed.

5 Benefits of Setting Study Goals

We all know that to be successful in our studies, or in any kind of endeavour, we need to "keep our eyes on the prize", as Bob Dylan used to say. We all know setting goals are important, having a system is important, yadda yadda yadda...

I'm sure you've heard it all before. And certainly, for it to be such a common advice means that there must be some truth and certainty to it, right? Of course. The most valuable gems sometimes come from the simplest advices. If you're still aren't pumped to set study goals, here are 5 benefits in doing so:

1. It shows definite results and shows it faster, period.

When you're laser-focused doing tasks that help bring you closer to what you envision as your end result, you achieve success at an ACCELERATED pace. Goals can definitely yield MASSIVE RESULTS if you're focused on driving through with MASSIVE ACTION.

2. Goals create urgency

People like to quantify stuff. In the working world, you're largely measured based on KPIs (Key Performance Indicators), many of which are based on a certain benchmark and within a certain period (for example, achieve 20 sales within a month). If you don't reach your KPIs consistently, you may not be considered for promotion or even be the first few to be retrenched during a company downsize.

It's easy for the company to do so because they can produce your KPI reports and show that you're under-performing and unproductive. This is why you're forced to do, do and do every day even when you don't feel like it.

THE A LISTER

Of course, we're not saying that you should keep yourself on your toes all the time when it comes to studying, but the process of keeping score with yourself on certain benchmarks will indicate where you've fallen short, and get them sorted quickly instead of procrastinating.

3. Once completed, they are a cause to celebrate!

Who says goal setting shouldn't be fun? As a student, I understand studying is tough. It takes effort and isn't exciting at all.

The thing is, after accomplishing their goals, many students don't go all out and celebrate enough! I guess you've heard of "Study hard and play hard".

Really, I had to use this overused phrase because we need it more than we can imagine. Don't just take one day to have fun at Resorts World Sentosa, take a whole well-deserved week devoted to having fun and not touching your books for that week.

4. Goals set you up for failure

Let's face it. There is a 50% chance (or more) of failing to achieve your goals. Consider the goals you've set over the last couple of years of your education. How many could you even remember actually doing and staying on track for a long time? Exactly. This is something many people don't realize when it comes to goal setting and goal planning. We think that just by using goals, we can definitely succeed in achieving our end result 100% of the time. In reality, your goal is never fool-proof and will disappoint you more times than you can ever imagine.

However, the beauty of goal setting is that you can structure them in a way such that you minimize this risk of failure, while allowing some wiggle room to change your plans if necessary.

Also, with failure comes wisdom. Goals allow you to re-evaluate your actions, and see what can be done better.

Life is always a learning process, and you may not always do something the first time right. It is through evaluation that you know what works, and what doesn't, and make changes to your goals so that you eventually get to where you want to go.

5. Goals show you the practical aspect of success

By creating goals, you create your blueprint (or outline) to realizing your vision. You create REAL, ACTIONABLE steps you need to take in order to succeed. It's like having a map that leads you to the hidden treasure chest.

How To Set Study Goals That Work?

By now, you already know that goals are the map to academic achievement. But the question now is, how do I set goals that work for me?

Before you set any kind of goal, you need to go through 3 simple, but critical steps to ensure that your goal leads you to where you want to go.

1. Identify the **problem**.
2. Identify the **destination**.
3. Identify the **solution**.

THE A LISTER

STEP 1: IDENTIFY WHAT STUDYING PROBLEMS YOU WANT TO GET SOLVED TODAY

Get out a sheet of paper and a pen, and draw a horizontal line down the middle of the piece of paper.

On the left side, start writing down what problems you face in your studies.

What study challenges do you want to solve now? What obstacles or problems do you want to eliminate now? Start writing them down line by line on your piece of paper.

You may have 5 or 10 problems you'd like to solve, just take the top 3 problems and write it down. Take about 5 minutes to do this exercise. You shouldn't take any longer than that.

Done? Now let's move on to the right side of that sheet of paper.

STEP 2: IDENTIFY WHAT YOUR END RESULT WILL LOOK LIKE

On the left side are your problems that you want to solve. On the right side will be the end result or destination you will get after you have successfully reached your goal.

Flesh it out in great detail how you want your end result to look like. Don't be vague, be specific. For example, if your problem is finding Chapter X of World History difficult to understand, your end goal might be to successfully describe 3 of 4 of the scenarios in Chapter X without referring to your notes. Similarly, do not spend more than 5 minutes here.

By now, you should already have filled up both sides of your piece of paper. It should look something like this now...

Problems	*End Result*
1. XXXXX	1. XXXXX
2. XXXXXX	2. XXXXXX
3. XXXXX	3. XXXXX

STEP 3: IDENTIFY HOW YOU ARE GOING TO GET THERE

What solutions can you come up with to overcome those problems? You don't have to write a whole paragraph of how you're going to do it. Just one simple statement or solution will do.

It could be using the "Make A Story" technique to remember the details of the battle scenes in Chapter X or committing to make mind maps and revising them once per week till the World History examinations.

Great job! You now have a rough game plan to boot! Now, let's take your goal and see how we can make it even better.

THE A LISTER

Tips to Supercharge Your Game Plan

There is a simple acronym professional goal setters will always use to ensure that their goals are clear and actionable, and it is called setting SMART goals.

S – Specific

M – Measurable

A – Attainable

R – Relevant

T – Time-bound

Specific

Being specific is being laser-sharp with our goals. We need that in order to succeed because it gives us focus and clarity. Without specificity, we're like a hunter that's blindfolded and is shooting arrows without the ability to look for the target.

How to be specific?

Don't state that you want to get 'A's in exams. Instead, state how many 'A's you want to get and in which subjects. Even better, state the amount of marks you want to get for each grade.

Being specific doesn't just apply to the end result, it could also apply to how you are going to make that goal work.

Measurable

There's a saying, "You can't improve what you don't measure", and that's really true.

How do you know if you are on the right track? By

measuring your progress. Each time an assignment or test result comes back to you, be sure to note it down and see if you have improved or not.

Having a trackable goal also means you know where you stand and how long or how much more effort it will take to reach your end destination.

Attainable

Your goal should be not too sky-high and unreachable, nor should it be too low that you don't have to put in effort to achieve it. Attainable means it should stretch your potential and your limits so that you feel challenged, but also, you feel with just the right effort and consistency, you can reach it.

However, if you're very ambitious like me, you might want to let loose on this one a bit. I personally go by the mantra of "go big or go home.

When you dare to dream big, your capacity for success increases and you are no longer limited by your own beliefs.

Most successful people achieve what they have achieved because they dare to dream big and take big actions to get the things they want in life.

A wise teacher once said, "Create a dream so big, so much so that it scares you. If it doesn't scare you, it's not big enough."

So, reach for the moon! If you don't catch it, at least you'll land among the stars. If you just reach for the clouds in the sky, you either reach it or you'll fall back to where you are right now.

Relevant

Every goal you set must be in alignment with your values and your purpose. In essence, your goals are just stepping stones for you to reach your purpose, that's all. The question you should ask yourself is... will this goal get me towards where I want to go? There is no point setting a goal to outdo all your other peers in Calculus if in fact, the main thing that's pulling you down is Physics.

Time-Bound

All goals should have a deadline. Having a deadline or time limit is a great way to motivate yourself to work on your goal every day because it creates urgency. Without such urgency, procrastination sets in. Not having a deadline tells your mind "Oh, I can leave this for another day". However, don't set too unrealistic deadlines and when you absolutely must, be flexible with your deadlines, so that you don't feel stressed out and lose the drive to study.

Two Common Mistakes in Goal Setting

1. Wording it Negatively

One of the largest and most common mistakes people make in setting goals is to word them negatively.

For example, many beginner goal-setters want to "stop procrastinating". That is their goal. However, they don't realize that this goal puts the emphasis on procrastination and subconsciously, their mind picks up the word "procrastination", and focuses on it. And what you focus on, increases. This is why many people who set weight-loss goals or getting out of debt goals fail to follow through because they keep focusing on the words "weight" and "debt".

"What you focus on expands, and when you focus on the goodness in your life, you create more of it." - Oprah Winfrey

So, instead of setting a goal "not to fail" or "stop procrastinating", set a goal to "ace my exams" or "get disciplined and focused on studies".

2. Expecting to Achieve Your End Result Perfectly

Let's say you set a goal to raise your scores from 68/100 to 88/100 in a test, and you do all the action steps and memory techniques you need to do to achieve that goal. And then, when the test results come back, you found that you scored a 75/100 for the test. Do you get upset and disappointed that you didn't achieve your goal? Or do you jump for joy and realize that you've made a 7-point improvement from the previous test?

Although you think you'll get the second reaction, you'll will most probably have the first reaction and beat yourself up for only getting a mere 7-point improvement, while you compare your test results with your peers who scored way better than you did. It's human nature.

The truth is, although we've set a clear and definite end point we want to achieve, sometimes we just can't predict what's going to happen in a test or exam. There might be a moderation downwards, the teacher couldn't read your handwriting clearly and decided to take away a few marks, or you just couldn't keep up with your goal and did the best you could.

The end result is our ideal destination. If we achieved it, great. If we didn't, but we've improved from the last time, it is also a reason to celebrate. Every improvement deserves a pat on the back, and that is what the next strategy is all about.

THE A LISTER

Activity: Is Your Goal S.M.A.R.T.?

If you have followed the 3-step goal setting exercise few pages ago, you'd have a solid outline of what you want and how to get there. Now, it's time to pack it with a punch!

Remember, your goals need to pass the SMART test.

- S – Specific ----------------------------- ❏
- M – Measurable ----------------------- ❏
- A – Attainable ---------------------------- ❏
- R – Relevant ------------------------------ ❏
- T – Time-bound ------------------------ ❏

Steps after that...

Goals cannot be achieved if they're just purely lip (or pen) service. Action steps need to be taken. Here's a summary of how to plan that:

1. Write your goal down on a sheet of paper in clear detail, fulfilling the SMART principle.

2. Set a deadline and sub-deadlines if necessary.

3. Identify the challenges you'll likely face, and find the most important one.

4. Identify the skills you need to overcome that challenge and focus on training that skill.

5. Identify the people who can help you achieve your goal. Think specifically about who and how to get their help.

6. Create a list of everything you will need to do to achieve your goal. Add to the list as many things you can

possibly think of.

      7. Organize them by priority and sequence. Design it in a checklist style if you prefer.

      8. Every day, focus on one single task to complete for that day. If the task takes more than a day, split the task up into sub-tasks, or part 1, 2, 3, etc...

      9. Every week (and month), check back to your original goal on your sheet of A4 paper and see whether you have been progressing towards it or not. Ask yourself if you have run off course anywhere during the week, and plan to correct your course in the following week's daily goals.

      10. Most importantly, have fun with it, and celebrate once you've hit your goal!

THE A LISTER

STRATEGY #5
Progression, Not Perfection

"Strive for continuous improvement, instead of perfection

*- Kim Collins,
100-metre sprint World Champion*

Many students suffer from the pressures of society to be perfect.

We are pressured to be perfect in sports, perfect in our schoolwork, perfect in communicating with other people, perfect in art, perfect in playing the piano, perfect in everything by the time we leave school. And, this seems especially so in Asia. According to a report in 2010, India has one of the highest suicide rates in the world, with around 51% being graduates, college students, or younger. The main reason for ending their lives point to the pressure to excel in school.

South Korea, which has one of the best education systems in the world, also sees such worrisome statistics.

There is definitely something that needs to be radically changed in the focus of education. However, what can we do right now, as students?

Instead of striving for perfection, we should strive for progression. As students, we are here to learn, and learning is a constant work-in-progress, for as long as we live. When we understand that, we take the stress and pressure off being perfect, and just focus on what our purpose is and ignore all of the competitiveness and noise out there.

That is why your purpose is so important. Learning needs to be driven internally, not from external circumstances and societal pressures.

I used to have a perfectionist frame of mind back in my secondary school and polytechnic days. I had a high regard and expectation for my ability and I was so determined to prove it to others through work that I considered "perfect". This caused me much stress and pressure, that led to a weak immune system and following that, I got ill.

After understanding that it was all about progression and not perfection, it took a lot of the pressure off my back and I began to enjoy learning even more. As famed scientist Albert Einstein once said, "Strive not to be a success, but rather to be of value."

But, with that being said, it is not an excuse to slack on your studies! As with everything you want in life, you need to work to achieve it.

The 10,000 Hour Rule

Progression is all about making improvements, practicing, and keep trying and failing until you succeed. In Malcolm Gladwell's book "Outliers", he studies highly successful people and notes that the reason for their success is because they have practiced their craft for an average of ten thousand hours until they've gained mastery from it.

THE A LISTER

He also claims that if you practice something for ten thousand hours, you'd also achieve a level of performance or skill close to perfection.

Now, I'm not saying that you should spend ten thousand hours studying a particular subject or practicing your memory techniques, but the meaning behind it is that you have to practice!

If you want to progress in your learning and get those 'A's you deserve, you need to practice. If you've created mnemonics, stories or mind maps as you have learned in Strategy #2, you need to constantly revisit them until you can recall them at the back of your head.

Practice takes time and a lot of hard work. Most students don't have the perseverance and give up at this stage. I hope you're not one of them!

You Don't Know What You Don't Know

Progression is also about discovering the things you don't know. This short, but profound, statement "you don't know what you don't know" tells us that we think we know everything...but we really don't. And, we don't even realize that we don't!

How scary is that?

People say that knowledge is power. And in the academic context, it really is. But the problem is, do we know everything we need to know? How can we find out?

If we don't even know what information or skills we're lacking in, how can we move closer to our ideal results? It's like immediately wanting to embark on a hike up Mount Everest after buying all the expensive climbing equipment and getting training.

You'd think you know everything about climbing Everest now that you've gone through training, but what's scary is only realizing you've overlooked the fact that your drinking water had become ice in the middle of your climb and you have no water left to drink!

In Alexander Pope's famous poem, An Essay on Criticism, he writes that, "a little learning is a dangerous thing" because people usually just listen to what they think they need to know and just like in the story above, when we find out we lack something, it's usually a little too late.

Luckily, a simple solution exists. If you have problems, chances are, others already have experienced the same problems and solved it. Your task is to simply find those experts out there who have already solved the same or similar problems, and learn from them.

"The shortest route to success is simply to follow someone who has already travelled that route"

So, if your goal is to score 'A's on your exams easily and consistently, find out who those top students are that have already done it. Ask them questions. Follow what they do. Think like them. Get advice from them. And learn from their mistakes.

If you want your results to be different than what you are getting right now, you'll have to start taking a different set of actions.

The Four Stages of Competence

In any kind of learning, you'll bound to go through four stages of progress. Known as the "conscious competence learning model", this model is incredibly simple to understand, yet it takes real determination to work your way through the

THE A LISTER

four stages. Knowing this model can help you, as a student, understand how all of us learn and avoid giving up halfway when you feel like you are going nowhere.

The model describes how a student goes from pure ignorance to purposeful mastery of any skill or any subject:

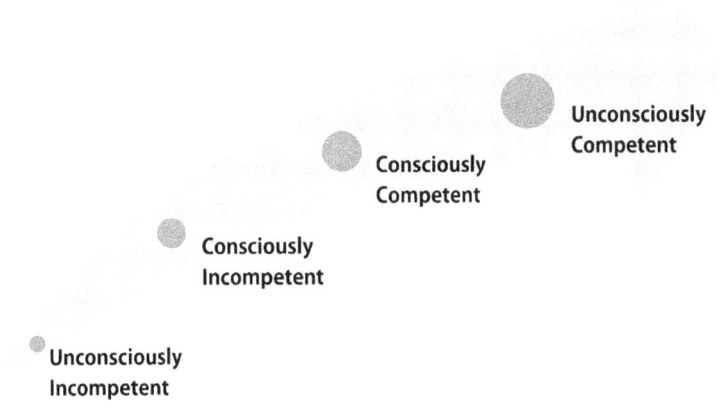

Stage 1: Unconsciously Incompetent

Remember our aspiring Everest climber? He had been in this stage and circling around it not knowing how unprepared he was for his climb! Unfortunately, this is really what happens to most people. They are completely unaware of how bad they are at something, and in many instances, actually thinks that they are pretty good at it! This prevents them from moving on to the next stage of learning, where the real learning begins.

Stage 2: Consciously Incompetent

In this stage, a student finally accepts the fact that there is more to it than meets the eye. This usually comes as a reality shock for the student after he gets disappointing results on his tests or exams.

He now knows that there are so many things in his subject matter or skill in which he hasn't been exposed yet, and wants to start getting familiar with it. However, he is usually overwhelmed by the fact that there are tons of things to learn, and doesn't know where to start.

In fact, you probably are at this stage right now! The fact that you're reading this book means that you accept the fact that you still have room to improve and are willing to learn. However, it is also at this stage where many people get intimidated and give up.

Stage 3: Consciously Competent

At this stage, you'd have already taken that step of faith to acquire the knowledge you need, and are working hard at it. You become more adept at whatever you do (you might even begin seeing results!) and learning becomes easier as you progress.

Stage 4: Unconsciously Competent

Here is where the skill or subject you're learning seems like a breeze. This is where most professional and internationally competing athletes' are, and is commonly referred to as "the zone".

The skill or subject becomes so easy and has become an everyday part of you. You may even be able to help your friends solve their homework problems without even referring to your study materials!

So, armed with this model, honestly ask yourself which stage you are at right now, and decide that you are going to stay the course to reach the stage of unconscious competence.

THE A LISTER

Activity: The Net of Imperfection

There is something that you should know about this book. This book had been re-written three times before it had finally been the physical product that you're holding in your hands today. Each detail, from the book cover to the sub-title, had been modified at least once. So you see, I too, had been a perfectionist.

After being introduced to this concept mid last year, I began to realize how unproductive I was in the whole process. I had been spending so much time being "right" that I totally lost my initial direction – which is to help students improve their grades using proven methods and strategies.

Then, in just a record of one and a half months, I completed my book, focusing only on adding value and not so much on being "right". Of course, there are so many things this book could be better in – delivery, graphics, content, promotion – but I now take the approach step-by-step, and not being perfect. Imagine, if I kept focusing on being "right and perfect" this whole time, this book would never have seen the light of day!

To get you in the "progression-rather-than-perfection" frame of mind, I have developed a poster for you, called the "Net of Imperfection™".

This Net represents your life. In making a net, several ropes are knotted together in a criss-cross fashion, revealing spaces in between them. These spaces are the imperfections in life. However, does that mean the net is unable to be used to catch fish? No!

As the fisherman hauls the net up from the sea, water flows away from the net, leaving behind an abundant catch.

Life is just like that. You don't need to be perfect and fill in all those empty spaces; you already have the ability in you to achieve great things.

Just focus on catching the fish, progress each step of the way, and leave all the unnecessary drama, distractions and things that don't serve you (i.e. the water) out.

Get the "Net of Imperfection" poster and place it somewhere where you'll look it every single day to remind yourself to progress instead of being perfect. A larger copy of the "Net of Imperfection" poster can be downloaded at **www.thealisterbook.com/netofimperfection**

THE A LISTER

STRATEGY #6
The Truth About Being Competitive

"Real learning comes about when the competitive spirit has ceased"

— Jiddu Krishnamurti,
Author & Philosopher

Competitiveness seems like a really hot topic in this day and age. Everyone just seems so bent on winning, and defeating others in the process. We always talk about competition – how two students are fighting for the top spot in the school, how we need to compete to get the job we want...

It seems as though we can only go forward when we kick someone else's behind. What kind of logic is that?

To be brutally honest, our one and only competitor we are fighting against in life is **OURSELVES**! We can lie to ourselves and say that other students who are "smarter" than us have taken our opportunity to get a scholarship or be on the Dean's list.

If you truly believe that, then the inner enemy has won. It has succeeded in preventing you from being the best that you are in your studies. Not only that, I can bet you the inner voice that's saying "You will never be able to do it" has also succeeded in stopping you from achieving in other areas of your life!

If you keep thinking in your mind that there are so many intelligent students "way up there" and you'll need to really fight your way to rise to the top with them, then your focus is out of whack. This is where society "tricks" you into believing that you have to fight to strive to the top.

You would always be fearful that you wouldn't be as capable as the top students, so you fight.

After days and months of thinking you're in a struggle, you will eventually burn out. So you see, this is a trap many hardworking and hopeful students fall into.

This is also what American author, Dr Wallace Wattles, calls the competitive frame of mind.

What the 1% don't want you to know

The secret to be ahead of the competition and potentially get to the top of your game is to create success instead of competing for success. Making the shift from the competitive plane onto the creative plane, in Dr Wattles' terms.

Quoting from his book, Dr Wattles mentioned that "You are to become a creator, not a competitor; you are going to get what you want, but in such a way that when you get it every other man will have more than he has now."

Isn't that powerful.

Many times, we get caught up in wanting to outdo others that we lose sight of what our goals are. We get into a mindless chase to be the best, but the question you have to ask yourself is, "Is what I'm striving for aligned with my 'Why'"?

THE **A LISTER**

To be a successful student doesn't mean being the best among everyone and in everything. It's to be better than the student you were yesterday.

What does it mean to create, though? Learning is a creation in itself. We create knowledge in our heads, we create by picking up useful skills that we didn't have before, and we create value for others by applying our knowledge and offer solutions that solve critical problems in society.

And, in the process of all of these, we create our life and our destiny.

I am always inspired by arts and music students because they are always motivated by the desire to achieve and fulfil their purpose, which is to CREATE beautiful pieces of work so that others may enjoy them. There is rarely any mention for the desire to beat others.

To decide to live on the creative plane instead of on the competitive plane will really make a big shift in how you see your academic pursuits. I know it did for mine.

This concept of "creating" is not a myth. One real-life example I could offer is the ubiquitous company known as Apple.

Apple is presently one of leading dominators in the global smartphone market, at the time of writing. And it owes it success to its constant innovation and value creation. Apple launched the iPhone back in 2007, the first-ever smartphone with a multi-touch interface.

The secret to its success was not because it was the first smartphone to be out in the world (In fact, smartphones such as the Palm Treo were in the market long before Apple released the iPhone), but because Apple put customers first and delivered what they wanted in a phone.

They CREATED value for customers by offering them a phone that's easy to use, sleek in design, innovative in software and great in their customer service.

So as you see, getting ahead of the competition isn't about beating others, as mainstream media would've liked you to believe.

Winning is not a zero-sum game. It doesn't mean that in order for you to get what you want, someone else has to lose.

Creation goes past all that and says, "When I win, everyone else wins."

So, the lesson to take away from this part is to actively seek ways to create your own successes rather than competing for them. What could you do right now in your school to create instead of compete?

Maybe you're competing for "A"s in a project-based assignment. Everyone's struggling to come up with the best proposal and report. Instead of focusing on the competition, focus on how you can create an impact in your project by coming up with a short skit, delivering a masterful presentation or writing up a proposal that will leave your lecturer in awe.

Don't do what 99% of your peers are doing. See how you can mix things up, and really think out of the box. When you disrupt the normal pattern of doing things, you differentiate yourself from the crowd, and that, my friends, is how you create an identity for yourself, create attention and awareness of the message you're trying to bring across, and that significantly increases your chances of being academically successful.

The sky is the limit as to how far your creativity goes in

THE **A LISTER**

creating success for yourself.

The Student Who Gave A Killer Presentation

I don't know if you've seen this clip before, but it has been making its rounds on the Internet.

Tarun Shakyawar, a student at Pune's Symbiosis Institute of Business Management in India, was faced with a common predicament among all students – he had to prepare a class presentation on the (oh, so boring) topic of 'Innovative HR Practices' in less than an hours' time and deliver it.

In that hour, he came up with an ingenious idea of singing his entire presentation in the tune of Linkin Park's 'In The End'.

Scan To View The Viral YouTube Video Now!

As a result, the entire class started singing along and it was such a huge hit that it went viral all over the Internet, and was even featured on sites like Buzzfeed and The Huffington Post! (I bet he scored amazing grades just for that)

How's that for tapping into your creative frame of mind?

How Losing the Competition Made Him Millions

You've definitely heard of Paypal, one of the largest online payment systems in the world. It's founder, Peter Thiel, had been a fierce competitor since young.

As an adolescent, Thiel competed to be one of the highest-ranked under-21 Chess Master players in the United States. As a student, he competed to get into the prestigious Stanford University. Then, he competed to get into Stanford Law School. Out of school, he further competed to become a clerk for a federal judge. Peter Thiel managed to win all these competitions with great success.

Then, he went on to compete for a Supreme Court clerkship. He was one of the few clerks who had made it to the interview stage. It was one of the greatest achievements if he had gotten the nod, he would be set for life. He was close to winning that last competition. But alas, Thiel lost the clerkship.

It was one of the first and biggest losses in his personal and professional life. So, instead of being a clerk, he went on co-founding Paypal and later on, sold Paypal to eBay, receiving around US$55 million for his stake in the company.

Years after, Thiel reconnected with an old friend from Stanford Law School, who remarked, "So, aren't you glad you didn't get that Supreme Court clerkship?"

THE A LISTER

What seemed like a great opportunity lost, was in reality, a blessing in disguise. At the time, it seemed like the only choice was to win the competition, or go home a failure. But life, as we know it, is very unpredictable. Imagine if he had won the clerkship, there wouldn't be a Paypal today and he would still be competing doggishly till this day while earning far less than what he has now.

Following that loss, Thiel mentions that "We often shouldn't seek to be really good competitors. We should seek to be really good [creative] monopolists." In our dog-eat-dog society, we often think that whoever competes the hardest comes out a winner. We sometimes do it just to give ourselves an ego-boost or so that others would respect us even more. But, we seem to be losing sight of what's "of value" in the bid to become more competitive.

Being a 'creative monopolist', in our context, means striving to be the only logical choice that others trust, one who delivers work of a high quality and thinks out of the box, and one that others look for if they need help. And, that can only be achieved by being creative and adding value to everything that you do.

In essence, don't focus on competition. Focus on how to become a 'creative monopolist' in your projects or schoolwork, so much so that you stand out from the rest of the crowd.

The Reason Why Are We So Competitive

We are conditioned from young to be competitive. Remember when you were a child you'd race with other children to see who was the fastest. When you won, you felt great. All the other kids would look up to you in awe and glory. When you weren't the fastest, especially when you had lost by a split second, you probably felt terrible and a burden to the rest. Your parents would've assured you that you weren't the slowest in the world, but deep inside, you still felt you could've done much better.

In the Asian context, many parents compare their kids' grades with other kids' and make a remark (or even reprimand them) if they scored lower than his other peers.

The desire to win is developed from such experiences since young. You know winning makes you feel fantastic, while losing makes you feel unworthy. For the most part, our competitive nature is really through social conditioning.

In class, the students who scored the highest in the spelling test would get sweets, while the students who didn't do well got a dressing down from the teacher (and his parents) and had to stay back for extra lessons.

At family gatherings, if you weren't the brightest among your cousins, you'd be compared to and lectured for not studying harder. This is especially so in a country like Singapore, where people queue overnight just to be the first in the country to get their hands on the new iPhone that's just released.

Competitiveness Is a Result of Feeling Lack

The root cause of us being competitive is an innate fear of not having enough. We often think there is not enough to

THE A LISTER

go around so we have to get it before someone else does.

It is a learned behaviour. We are taught since young that there's not enough and we have to compete for our share. For example, when you see someone else having a lot of money, do you feel there's less money in the world for you to be rich? When you see your classmates get "A"s during a test, do you automatically assume you have a lesser chance of getting an 'A' because all the "A"s are completely given out? This scarcity thinking is ingrained in our brains since our childhood but it is possible to "unlearn" it.

We feel lack because we think that the Earth's resources are limited, money in the world is limited, and opportunity or success in the world is limited. Someone has to lose before we can win. This zero-sum game is played over and over in our competitive world that we don't stop to think how else to "win" other than beating others.

In fact, the world is ever-more limitless and abundant than it was many years ago, and academic success is getting easier to achieve despite the seemingly increasing competition around us! We already have everything we need to achieve any goal and result in life!

In recent years people had been talking about how crude oil is expected to only last us around another 50 years and the media has painted a very catastrophic story for the oil production industry, and the entire world economy. That got many researchers, bankers and industry leaders panicky.

Today, we see a brighter story with the possibility of new, alternative sources of oil like shale oil and tar sands being extracted easily and at a low cost. Where there seems to be no way left, a way will be found.

You Already Have Everything You Need to Be An 'A' Lister!

Despite what you believe, you don't need extra tuition, you don't need more money, you don't need more studying than what is sufficient, you don't need more luck and you definitely don't need a brain transplant (I believed I needed it in the past).

You already have all the resources, brain capacity and luck you need to get the results you want! You have to believe that, because if you don't, you'll return to the thinking of lack and scarcity, which will bring you back to the competitive plane.

The Hidden Genius in You

In 1854, a young boy with hearing difficulties attended public school in Port Huron of Michigan. This lad was a hyperactive kid, and he could not keep still in class for more than a minute. His teachers remarked that he was "too stupid to learn anything", and he was pulled from school after three months there.

Today, he is remembered as a "genius" who had greatly impacted the world. This brilliant man was Thomas Edison. He was best known as the inventor of the electric light bulb, but had many other world-changing inventions such as the phonograph and the movie camera.

THE A LISTER

He did not believe he lacked intelligence, despite being labelled "stupid". He did not believe he lacked "luck" despite being unable to get the light bulb to work over 10,000 times. Thomas Edison believed that he did not lack anything, but had everything in the world to become successful.

Many students believe success is conditional. That means, only when all the resources are aligned, and the conditions are right, will they attain academic success. They are waiting for that perfect time when they have all the resources they need – be it energy, time, motivation or intelligence – so that they have one shot of making it to the top. They don't realize the perfect time has always been here, so they keep on waiting. 'A' Listers know this, and so they make use of every chance to inch toward their academic goals. 'A' Listers know that opportunities are not discovered, they are created.

You must relinquish the thought that getting an 'A' depends on circumstances external to you. You should not blame your family background, financial situation, illnesses, friends, study environment, teachers or anything for your past results. No matter what your situation is, you have everything you need **RIGHT HERE AND RIGHT NOW**.

No use hoping that you'll wake up with a super-memory so that you'll do well in the future. You have to believe that you already have the best set of brains in the world, and get to work using it effectively. This is the effect of having a mindset fixed on success, and it's what I will be sharing with you in Strategy #10.

A Final Note on Competitiveness

Now, I'm not saying to "stop being competitive". In fact, competition is necessary for growth and improvement. Without competition, prices of smartphones would be soaring well over tens of thousands of dollars, and we wouldn't have as many variations and varieties of fast food as we have today!

However, what I'm advocating is instead of FOCUSING on competition and winning, FOCUS on creating as much knowledge and value as possible.

Competition will always be there whether we like it or not. To go against competition is not working smart. To take a different approach in looking at competition, is.

THE A LISTER

Activity: Embrace Your Competition

It's easy for us to get envious, or even jealous of our peers, when they score better grades than us. This is a common response that many students will have.

However, in the "creative" zone, there is no reason to. Think of it this way, would you rather have friends who you consider "losers" and do not accomplish much, or would you rather have friends who are inspiring to you because they are great students, and you're lifted higher because of what you learn from them?

Instead of being envious, learn to live vicariously through the actions of your 'A' Lister peers.

Here's what you can do:

When a friend gets fantastic grades for a test or exam, instead of making snide remarks or gossiping, give them their due credit and say one of the following (or the like),

- *"Great work! I'm so proud of you. Your efforts have paid off!"*
- *"Well done! I'm so happy for you!"*

When celebrating someone else, mean what you say. Don't be condescending or sarcastic. Really mean it!

If you say you're happy for a friend, be truly happy for them! If you say you're excited for their achievements, jump for joy along with them!

Such positive energy will rub off on you, and soon enough, you'll find that you'll be the one being celebrated!

By doing this, you've automatically flipped yourself from the competitive frame-of-mind to the creative frame. Then, all you got to do is to stay in that frame, by creating knowledge and adding value to your work and to others.

THE A LISTER

STRATEGY #7

The Art of Thinking Critically

"The important thing is to never stop questioning"

- Albert Einstein,
US (German-born) Physicist

Many people have heard the great name of Socrates at some point in their lives. However, not many would know who he actually is, apart from knowing that he was a Greek philosopher.

Socrates was born in Athens, the capital of Greece, in a humble family. A strong believer of knowledge and wisdom, he sought to answer difficult life questions like "What is beauty?", "What are ethics?" Knowing that he couldn't answer it himself, he went around his town in Athens asking these questions to the people he came across.

Some said they were busy. A few gave brief responses, but ultimately, many people ignored him.

When Socrates got such responses, he would try to suggest them to think deeper by asking them more questions and challenging them to see flaws in their logic. This made the some of the townsfolk angry, and even threatened to beat him up.

The few who found interest in his way of thinking eventually became his followers. The townsfolk, unsurprisingly, were angered by what he was teaching the young people of Athens, and soon after, he was to be sentenced to death for "corrupting the youth" and not respecting the gods. Although he died an unjust death, he left behind a legacy for his followers, and greatly influenced the advent of Western philosophy.

The Magic of A Question

One thing we can learn from Socrates is that he always asks questions and tries to explore deeper into a specific idea or thought. When you ask questions, you activate deeper levels of thought and this active learning helps you understand complex subjects and concepts much better.

When we actively receive information, and our minds are responsive to the information, the neurons in our brains begin to build links quickly and naturally. What this means is that you'll be able to recall the solution to your problem whenever you are faced with it again much more easily and in more detail, as compared to information taught in lectures.

Why is this so?

With lectures, communication is one-way. This means that you are passively listening, while the lecturer is actively providing the information by their presentations. When you ask a question, you are engaging in two-way communication. Both of you are actively involved in the flow of information. This flow helps to reinforce the information in your mind much more easily.

THE A LISTER

Writing Your Essays Easily

One of the well-known sayings of Socrates is "what I do not know, I do not think I know". Many times, our ego plays a big role in how much we learn. If we think we know something well, we tend to stop paying attention and "move on" to the next piece of information. If we don't know something well, we start making up ideas about the subject based on our own assumptions and a few pieces of information on the subject matter. We do it because it's usually difficult for anyone to admit that they're ignorant. That they simply "don't know".

Socrates had a great way to disallow the ego from doing that. By being constantly aware that he did not know many things, and strived to gain understanding, he stopped talking and started listening to what others were saying.

In your journey toward academic excellence, it is important to not only have your own opinions and arguments about a particular subject matter, but also to stay quiet and listen to the ideas and arguments others come up with, and seek to understand how and why they've come to that perspective of thought.

Always seek to ask someone (or yourself, if you're working on a paper), "How did you/I come to that conclusion?" or "If ... occurred, what would be the result?"

Not only is this useful when you're writing a paper, it is also helpful where you need to understand complex models, frameworks and theories. By asking such questions to yourself, like "What am I trying to find here?" or "What would be an example?" or "Why does this happen?" it will help you to identify whether or not you really know your stuff well.

Letting Go Of the Ego

One of the well-known sayings of Socrates is "what I do not know, I do not think I know". Many times, our ego plays a big role in how much we learn. If we think we know something well, we tend to stop paying attention and "move on" to the next piece of information.

When we learn to let go of our ego, we are ready to receive and absorb whatever new information we will receive.

"Your ego is not your amigo"

- Joel Bauer,
Mentor of Mentors, Master of Persuasion

THE A LISTER

Activity: Posing Questions

In your next lecture or class, bring a sheet of blank A4-sized paper along.

Pay attention to the lecture. While you're trying your best to understand the lecture, notice when your brain starts to come up with various questions about the content that you can't quite seem to grasp. Immediately write them down on your sheet of paper, in bullet-point form. You should have a list of questions ready for the lecturer by the end of the lecture.

At the end of the class, try to get a hold of the lecturer and start asking your questions. Be as specific as you can.

In your interaction with him or her, your mind may come up with even more specific questions. Direct each one of them to him or her, unless it is something that you are sure you'll be able to find the answer to on Google.

Something as simple as asking thoughtful questions to your lecturer might seem pretty easy, but many people just don't do it because they're afraid of coming across as "stupid", "a slow learner" or, they are just simply too lazy or embarrassed to do it.

Timothy Ferriss, the author of "The 4-Hour Workweek", is a master at this. If he ever received anything less than an 'A' on the first test of a given class, he would bring 2-3 hours of questions to the grader's office and not leave until he or she had answered all of them or stopped due to exhaustion.

Then on, the grader would think long and hard about giving him less than an 'A', unless he or she had good reasons for doing so. They knew Tim would definitely come knocking for another three-hour visit.

THE A LISTER

STRATEGY #8

New Strategies for 21st Century Students

"Victorious warriors win first and then go to war, while defeated warriors go to war first and then seek to win"

- Sun Tzu,
Author of *The Art of War*

Case Studies & Life Application Questions

The trend for schools and educational institutions in setting test questions goes toward real-life applications and case studies.

Now, more than ever, you as a student need to be able to learn to use the theory and concepts that you have learnt and apply it to real-world examples.

How do you score for these types of questions? Always remember that behind each question are a set of fundamental principles and concepts that are not likely to change. You just have to discern what the examiner is trying to test you on and then construct your answer such that it hits every bulls-eye.

For every kind of question, always ask yourself, "What is

the examiner trying to test me on?" Many times, the answer will be obvious when you dissect and carefully read through the question.

When you have figured that out, it's just like you have the examiners checklist in your mind. Now, you have to make sure the points that you've written in your answer tackles all the items on the checklist.

For Math-related questions, teachers like to change the numbers on the questions and word them a little differently. However, once you have practiced and understood how to solve such questions step by step, you will be able to tackle any of such similar questions, no matter how differently it is worded.

When in Doubt, Ask Google

In today's tech era where we are constantly being bombarded by information from everywhere, you can literally find an answer to any question that you can think of. In fact, if you've been on the Internet for some time, you must've seen memes where students give credit to Google, Copy and Paste, and Wikipedia for helping them graduate high school or college.

Any question that you've ever thought of has been asked

THE A LISTER

(and most likely, answered) on the Internet. And, that includes questions about your subject.

I personally am a big "Googler". I Google everything. From random questions that pop into my head, to finding out what caused those nagging headaches that won't go away. Also, any time I'm stuck with a concept or I can't seem to think of any ideas for a project, I use Google to give me some ideas. When you look hard enough, you can find some ideas that make you go, "Wow. Why didn't I think of that?" and when you present it to your teachers, they'll be equally wowed over by the level of thought and ingenuity in your project, which probably gets you an 'A'.

If you are having struggle with your schoolwork or didn't understand what your lecturer was saying when he was explaining a difficult concept such as String Theory, rely on Google to help you sort that out. The Internet is full of people who may teaching your particular subject, or have a full-time profession in your area of study. They are the experts to go to.

The Internet is a multimedia platform that caters to all learning types, so if you get bored reading a 5000-word article on how transistors work, you could watch a video that guides you through the process with demonstrations and verbal explanation. As I am a visual kind of guy, I'd hop over to youtube.com and key in the topic I need further clarification on. After one or two videos, I feel like an expert in that topic already!

The problem with most students is that they don't take full advantage of this technology. Many students ask their lecturers questions that can be easily answered with a simple Google search. Some students are get lazy or distracted when they visit YouTube, with all the funny cat videos and shows online.

I used to have trouble with Chemistry back in my Secondary School days. So, I hopped over to Youtube and found some amazing channels like Periodic Table of Elements and NurdRage, which showed these scientists blowing up things and explaining how the reaction works behind all of that. Besides, learning about the chemical reactions and the various concepts I needed help with, it also got me passionate about Chemistry, and that made me motivated to do well in this area.

Some of the resource sites that I go to are: YouTube, Khan Academy, PatrickJMT (Math – www.youtube.com/patrickjmt), Udemy practices and quizzes (www.udemy.com), flashcards online (StudyBlue Flashcards) and social sites (forums, interest groups).

One of the highly valuable skills in today's society, no matter where you go, is the skill of resourcefulness. Being resourceful means being able to find solutions to solve a problem quickly and easily. So, don't ditch your Googling skills too early…you may need it even more in the future!

Strive to Simplify

In our crazy and fast-paced world, people are increasingly finding the need to slow down and simplify. Go back to basics. This is true even for students. Why get stressed out over losing pages of notes from your textbook, when all you need is just a thin folder with all the information you need in it? Why bother wasting time keeping pages of old worksheets when all you need to do is extract the questions that you frequently get mistakes and practice them till you can answer them perfectly without looking at your notes? Why bog yourself down trying to rote memorize a concept when all you need to do is to use an analogy, stories or mnemonics?

THE A LISTER

Don't strive for sophistication and complication, strive to simplify. And, as Einstein always says, "Keep it simple, stupid!"

Read More & Read Widely

Those who know me know that I like to study how successful people achieve their success. Having read many books, attended many seminars and even met with a few of these successful people, I realize that they all are avid readers. They will certainly carry a book with them at all times, and read it when they have some spare time, wherever they are.

Successful people always keep learning. It is a never-ending learning process for them, and books provide instant wisdom and knowledge that the authors have taken years to become aware and learn of.

Don't become stuck to the opinion that you just need to know enough to pass your tests or exams. If you want to become an 'A' lister, you need to know at least 30% more than what your peers know!

You might ask, "What's the use of studying so much if it's not tested?"

You want to be able to know as much as you can about the subject matter so that you get a full picture of how it is being used in modern applications. By reading more on your topic, you will also have more examples you can use to understand the concept better. This creates more neural pathways in your brain, which means you will be able to remember and recall the topic better. Finally, it will possibly ignite your interest in the topic or subject even further and make you more passionate and driven to excel in it.

Back in my poly days, I would go to the library many

times to read more on my subjects, especially the ones I had trouble understanding or learning. And, the fact that I was one of the few conscientious students who made the effort already made the switch in my mind that I would be able to master this subject and be able to answer whatever questions related to it like a pro.

Share Your Knowledge with Others

It is said that the best way to learn something is to teach it to someone else. This cannot be any truer. I strongly believe in the Law of Reciprocity – which says that by what you give, you will be returned in kind. When you give out your knowledge unselfishly, you will receive the knowledge and help when you need it in return.

Don't be afraid to share your notes with others or spend time helping others on a topic they're stuck on. When you teach, your brain is retrieving and processing all the stored information you've learned and converting them into logical sentences when you speak. In effect, you are training your brain to locate where the information is exactly stored, so that it can retrieve it faster next time.

It's like remembering where you store your things in your bedroom. At first, you might have to spend some time digging for those old family photos you've kept 5 years ago. But once you've found it (the lower drawer next to the bed!), you'll zip there straight away whenever someone wants to have a look at the old pictures.

Scientific studies have shown that soon after you learn something, 80% of the information is quickly forgotten.

You might already know this fact that when we try to explain something you've learned to others, we store the information much better in our heads and recalling that information is much easier later on.

Most of the times, we seem to forget most of whatever we learnt in class. However, the truth is, the information is already captured in your mind, but hasn't been processed and organized so that you can recall it whenever you want to.

By teaching someone else that same information you learned, your memory is constantly being imprinted with that information. You're actively organising and refining those ideas so that you can communicate what you learned in your own words!

This forces you to mentally structure your understanding of the subject at hand so that you can relate it to someone else clearly, and this helps because you are now thinking of how to word your answer so that it's easily understood by your friends, and more importantly, the examiner, when you pen down that recalled knowledge onto the exam script.

"If you can't explain it simply, you don't understand it well enough" – Albert Einstein

When you explain a subject matter to someone else, you demonstrate your understanding of that subject matter.

Think about it, you can't be able to explain something with confidence and ease unless you absolutely know what you're talking about, right?

Model Top Students

Have you heard of the "Friends Effect"? The "Friends Effect" says that you are the average of the five people whom you spend most of your time with. We know since young that friends have a profound influence on our lives. To a great extent, they mould our thinking, our ideas, our habits and our behaviour.

If you want to score the grades that high-achieving students get, get with the high-achieving students and BE like them. This means to know how they think, how they behave and, critically, how they spend their time.

In Neuro-linguistics Programming, this is called "modelling". By modelling, we shape ourselves to be THEM (who we look up to and want to be like). It is a process that has been used by many of successful people we know today.

Warren Buffett, one of the highly-regarded investors and richest people in the world, modelled after his mentor and professor, Benjamin Graham. Benjamin Graham had been his idol ever since he picked up his book "The Intelligent Investor", and entered Columbia Business School as an undergraduate as he wanted to be taught by Graham, who was a professor there. After college, he even managed to work for Graham in his hedge fund partnership. Through his book and his lectures, Warren Buffett learnt a great deal about investing. Buffett even remarked that the book "was by far the best book about investing ever written". But, it was only through Buffett's personal encounters and working with Graham, did he learn how to use these ideas and concepts, mould it to form his own, and become the world's greatest investor of all time.

To model is **NOT** to be a perfect carbon copy of a person. It is really to find out the underlying factors that make a person successful and apply them to your life as it seems fit.

Picking Up Hints

As a 21st century student, you need to be able to know how to learn smart. Learning smart means knowing what topics are important, what to focus on and eliminating information that isn't worth your time studying on.

THE A LISTER

Many times, teachers and lecturers will give out hints. This is why it is so important to attend lectures and classes! By paying attention to lectures, you will know how to discern which areas of the lecture are important and which ones are not. Sometimes, lecturers may simply tell you which areas you need to focus on and are important. Sometimes, they will not tell you, but you can probably tell through a few tell-tale signs:

- Repeating the concept over and over, making sure everyone understands
- Talking pace slows
- Tone of voice deepens and becomes louder
- Giving plentiful of examples
- Asking for student responses

Many times, when a hint is being given out, you have to pay very close attention to what your lecturer is saying, and not simply "star" that particular topic. If he or she has a certain way of wording the topic that is different than the one in your book, your best bet is to use what your teacher has said to answer questions. It will seem "original", and your lecturer will award you marks because your answer is exactly what he or she is looking for.

Foods, Music and Apps to Study Better

There are many things you could do to overclock your brainpower and capacity that the top students many times admittedly do. Besides gulping down bottles of Essence of Chicken on your exam day, other foods can also help optimize your brain for better learning.

Brain Foods You Must Try

- Salmon
- Nuts and Seeds
- Avocados
- Dark Chocolate (!)
- Eggs
- Blueberries
- Tea

Apart from chunking down on chocolate and tea, music can make you smarter too. You can listen to any kind of music, contrary to popular belief, as long as it doesn't distract you from your work.

Music which has vocals in it can be a bit distracting, because you will likely concentrate on the lyrics rather than on your schoolwork. So, get a playlist of instrumentals or minus-one tracks.

If you still find yourself singing to the tunes in your head, get purely instrumental music. It doesn't have to be Mozart or Bach. Personally, I listen to a lot of jazz, blues and sax music. Chillout music also works great, and it relaxes you when you're studying! Some of my friends also have the likes for soundtracks – eg. Star Wars, Game of Thrones, Hans Zimmer – they all work fine.

THE **A LISTER**

SCAN THE QR CODE BELOW TO ENJOY A 2-HOUR STUDY & FOCUS MUSIC PLAYLIST

While you're sorting your music playlist on your phone, why not download a few apps that aid you in your studying? 'A' listers are techno-geeks. We always love to find a better and faster way to collect and organize information and get things done.

Here are a few apps that I personally use to organize my life as a student. All these apps can be found on the Google Play Store as well as Apple App Store, and best of all, they are FREE!

Wunderlist | www.wunderlist.com

Wunderlist is a to-do list that I use for anything and everything I need to remember to do. What's great about Wunderlist is its real-time sync function across all devices. That means you could update a to-do on your phone, and have it show up when you use your computer. Another cool feature that I really find useful is that you can have it as a widget on your Android's home screen. This means you can immediately know what's left to be done without having to wait for the app to open.

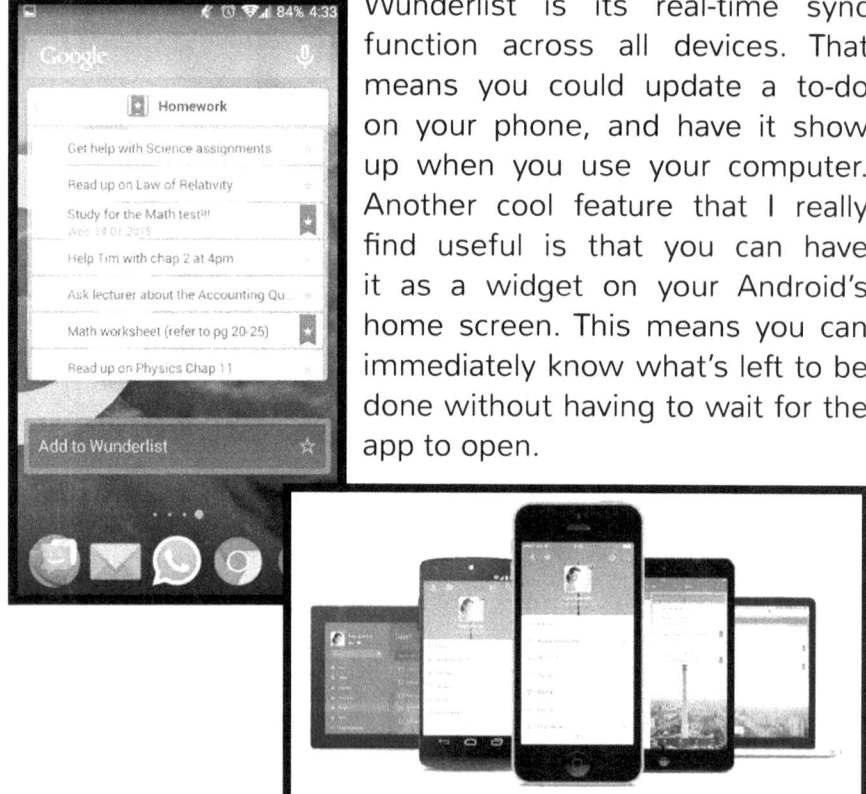

THE A LISTER

Evernote | www.evernote.com

When a to-do list is not enough, Evernote is here to help. For me, I like to think of Evernote as my "other brain". It's like a mass brain dump and storage facility where I can keep all my research materials and articles for projects, interesting articles for later reading and organize all my thoughts. It's a service anyone should have, whether you're a student or a professional.

Google Drive | www.google.com/drive

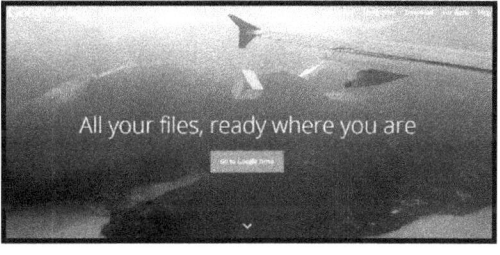

If you aren't using Google Drive yet, you're missing out. With 15 GB of storage space, Google Drive is the ultimate service that allows you to store your files, study materials, e-resources, and just about any personal stuff you have. For students who are working on their projects, it's a great tool because you can use the collaborate function to work on the same document at the same time! Say goodbye to sending countless emails around.

myHomework Student Planner | www.myhomeworkapp.com

myHomework is an awesome app that takes care of all the nitty-gritty of managing schoolwork. This app allows you

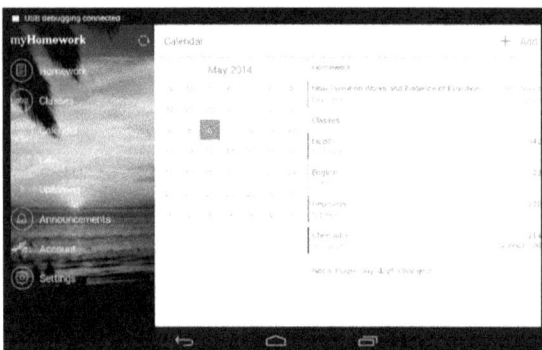

to input your class times, so that you always know where and when the next class is. You can also input reminders for your assignments and receive rewards for doing your homework! How cool is that!

Credits: www.myhomeworkapp.com

StudyBlue Flashcards | https://www.studyblue.com/online-flashcards

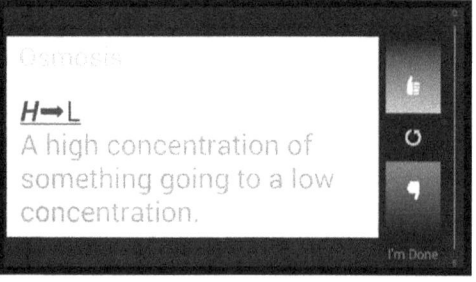

Flashcards allow you to master keywords in a fun and interesting way. With StudyBlue Flashcards, not only will you be able to learn more effectively, the app tracks what you get right and wrong, so you can spend your precious hours on material you've not yet gotten the hang of. What I also like about StudyBlue Flashcards are its study reminders that send you a text message when it's time to study. With this app, you could study anywhere, any time.

THE A LISTER

Practice Makes ...

Practice makes perfect, right?

We've been told since young that practice makes perfect, but in actuality, practice really only makes permanent. What do I mean by that?

We all believe that to get better, you need to practice. To get better at dancing, you need practice. To get better at Math, you need to practice. Many students do put in hours of practice, but end up getting disappointed because they didn't get the results they worked so hard for. So what's the catch?

What's missing is that you need to practice the right things. The right strategies. If you're constantly practicing, but you have the wrong facts or a strategy that doesn't work for you, you will keep getting the same results you are getting now, and wonder why you didn't improve. If you want to change your results, you got to change your methods. Practicing only makes you more skilled at what you are doing – be it it's the correct or incorrect thing.

If you keep solving the same problem incorrectly, identify it and change it until you have gotten it right. Then you start practicing.

In essence, don't practice your mistakes, practice your successes.

Handling Stress

Study stress is one common thing that all students can closely relate with. Even for myself, study stresses are one of the biggest hindrances that can cause my mind to go blank and my stomach to churn during tests or exams.

However, you can take control of stress by knowing why you are stressed in the first place. In the context of a student, the main cause of stress comes from not being prepared for a test or exam or project submission.

How can you be better prepared? Get all of your mind maps done weeks (or even months, if you can) before the exam. Start going through them at least one week prior to the examination. Know your mnemonics and stories well enough and without struggle. In the next strategy, I'll share with you more tips to get prepared for the final battle.

If you are stressed out, here are a few tips you can use to combat those stresses:

- Listen to relaxing music
- Take a short break & watch funny videos
- Write down your stressful thoughts
- Positive affirmations
- Practice deep, focused breathing from your diaphragm
- Talk to a friend or family member about it

THE **A LISTER**

Activity: Take 2!

There is no point knowing so many study strategies if you don't implement them to achieve the results you want.

Now that you have read through all the study tips in this chapter, pick 2 of them you think you will be able to implement.

It can be downloading and using a study app plus doing positive affirmation exercises when you're stressed, or it can be journaling stressful thoughts and grazing on nuts while studying.

Pick two and write it down here:

1) _____

2) _____

For the next one week, implement it like crazy! If you had written down that you would like to change your music playlist to a more study-friendly playlist, get working on finding those sweet tunes and loading it up each time you sit down for a study session.

Remember, change is the hardest during the beginning stages. Keep grinding, keep staying persistent.

After you've successfully completed the first week, continue with the next, and then the next…until it becomes so natural to you, and has become a part of your study routine.

THE A LISTER

STRATEGY #9

How to Survive Your Finals

"Exams + Facebook = Your head is in the wrong book!"

- Azgraybebly Josland

Cramming Doesn't Work

According to a survey conducted by the Indiana University of Pennsylvania, 99% of students cram for tests or assignments. It's a common thing to do among all students who struggle to squeeze every second out for studying nearing their finals. But cramming doesn't work, although you think it might.

When you cram, you trade in sleep time for study time. With lesser sleep, you become groggier, less alert and less focused on what you're studying, because your mind is constantly craving more sleep.

Also, because you know you have not enough time to

remember all the information you need, you get stressed out. Then, all you ever do is what I call "empty studying", you just look like you're studying and learning, but nothing ever goes into your head. These are the kinds of students who flip pages back and forth, and soaking the textbook in highlighter ink.

My advice, therefore, is to stop cramming and start doing from Day One. Plan your study schedules early. Space out your study periods. Make sure that all your mind maps and notes are ready weeks before the exam, and that you've revised your notes at least twice. And lastly, get sufficient sleep every night during the period of your exams!

Do Practice Papers

If you want to be an 'A' lister, this is a must.

There are so many advantages of doing past exam papers that it doesn't make sense not to do it. Even if you fail to implement everything else in the book, if you work on this tip repeatedly, you'll still see a marked jump in grades from your previous exams or tests.

Always try to get recent papers, as the questions will follow the updated syllabus and most examiners will set the papers you are sitting for by referencing the most recent past exam papers.

Be sure to time yourself when you're doing them. And, if possible, get the answer sheet for the paper so that you can easily assess your performance and learn the general marking style of the examiner.

In general, doing past exam papers:

- **Allows you to see which topics you are weaker at.** It provides instant feedback so that you focus on "brushing up" on the weaker topics. Furthermore, you can afford to make all the mistakes you want and learn from them, instead of making them during the actual paper.

- **Helps you improve on your timing.** You write more accurate answers, and in record time.

- **Gets you primed up on exam skills.** You will become more skilled in exam time management, understanding the mark scheme for that subject, being familiar with the style questions are set, and the format of the exam. This allows you to find out what things examiners are looking out for, and potentially score the maximum marks by giving them what they want.

You get your mind and body prepped to sit for two to three hours in one go, and improve your perseverance in writing continuously for that period of time.

Lastly, it builds up your familiarity to exam sitting and you become more self-confident.

Prepare to Conquer

To avoid feeling overwhelmed and stressed, make sure you've done all your preparation work. By preparation work, I mean noting down the dates and times of your exam, finding out the venue, packing exam stationery, having a full bottle of water to bring with you in the examination room and some sweets (if you always feel sleepy and can't stay alert).

Preparation also means having all the information you need to know at your fingertips. If you've studiously made your mind maps, mnemonics and practiced on past papers till you can confidently list out the key points or keywords for any possible kind of question, then you're all set and ready to go.

Having an Exam Ritual

An exam ritual is essential if you want to be an 'A' Lister. Ask any high achiever, they'll tell you that there are certain (quirky) things that they do before an exam. An exam ritual primes you up for success. ALL 'A' Listers know it works (for sure).

Look at any big sports players, they all have their own set of rituals they do before a tournament. Michael Jordan, the all-star Basketball player, always wore a pair of his North Carolina college shorts under his Chicago Bulls shorts in every game. The number one tennis player for women's singles, Serena Williams, also has some interesting pre-match rituals. For every game, she has to tie her shoelaces exactly in a certain fashion. Before each serve, Williams bounces the ball five times and on her second serve, twice.

Rituals make you feel comfortable, when the atmosphere is intense and stressful. When you perform your ritual, what you'll get is a clear mind, relaxed nerves and focus. You'll feel as if you're at the top of your game and in control – and this is very important. Half the battle is already won if you start of well by feeling energized and confident.

So, if you don't already have your own ritual, how do you go about creating one? There are a few popular (not weird) rituals that you can use to keep your mind primed for success:

Visualization

The practice of visualization is a very powerful ritual that you can do anywhere, and only takes a short time to complete. You could even do it five minutes before the exam and it will pull your motivation and focus up significantly.

In the case of exams, close your eyes and imagine

THE A LISTER

yourself successfully completing the exam, with so much more time to check through your answers thoroughly. Imagine yourself writing your answers with confidence and ease, and being masterful at what you do. See with your mind how easily words flow out of your pen, and imagine receiving back the marked script with plentiful red ticks at the sides. See the image of the blank area where the total marks are tabulated, and see it with a big red tick (or stars) and the marks you desire to attain.

Visualization is not simply new age "positive thinking". It is a technique that has been relied on for many years, and has always been used to train the top athletes for peak performance.

Many world-class athletes and successful people have used visualization to achieve what they want, including Tiger Woods, Arnold Schwarzenegger, Oprah Winfrey, Jim Carrey and even Will Smith.

The Power of Visualization

Broke and poor in 1987, Jim Carrey wanted so badly to become a world-renowned actor that he wrote himself a cheque for $10,000,000 (ten million dollars). He dated it 'Thanksgiving 1995' and added "for acting services rendered". He then placed the cheque in his wallet and looked at it each day. He would also drive to the street that many movie sets were filmed on and where Hollywood celebrities lived, and visualized directors and people he respected being interested in his work.

Just before 1995, Jim Carrey found out that he would be receiving $10 million dollars for his role in 'Dumb and Dumber'.

Deep Breathing

If you find yourself getting overly worked up and stressed out just right before the exam, deep breathing is one quick way you can bring yourself back to calmness and focus.

Close your eyes and focus on the ins and outs of your breath. Try to keep your focus on your breath, ignoring any distracting thoughts, sounds, formulas, definitions, mind-map images you might have. The idea is to keep your mind empty of all thoughts in this current moment.

Remember to breathe from your diaphragm, and not your lungs. This way, your breath becomes deeper and you'll feel more relaxed.

Prayers / Affirmations

Another popular way is to repeat prayers or affirmations to yourself silently. An affirmation is a positive statement that when repeated, get impressed into the subconscious mind over time. Some affirmations you may like to use include, "I will do well in this exam as I'm fully prepared", "I can ACE this exam without struggle", "I am a master at this" and "Today is the best day of my life".

THE A LISTER

Even heavyweight champion, Muhammad Ali, has been known to use affirmations, his most prominent line being "I am the greatest!"

8 Common Mistakes Students Make During Exams (And How You Can Avoid Them)

1. Not Checking Your Answers Thoroughly

It happens.

You finish a paper early with half an hour left to spare. At this point, many students make the mistake of submitting in their paper without looking through their answers at least once.

I recommend that once you've finished your paper, use that extra time to check through all your answers thoroughly, making sure that you haven't left anything out, and you're certain that you've answered every question as best as possible and you're satisfied with it.

And, by thoroughly, I mean really being meticulous with your checking. Being the OCD me that I am, I'll read through all my answers a minimum of two rounds, to make sure I didn't miss out anything on the first look through.

2. Leaving Blanks

This one is a very common mistake students make during exams and tests. You might lrave a question blank because you didn't know how to do it, or what to write.

Or, perhaps you skipped the question, hoping to come back to answer it after you've finished all the other questions, but didn't have the time to go back to it.

Whatever the case, always write something down. Even if you don't know the answer to it, look at the question and make a guess. Explain it in your own words. This way, you'll potentially be able to get at least a few marks, rather than getting none.

If you're answering a multiple-choice question, all the more you shouldn't be leaving blanks. If you can, rule out the choices you know are incorrect, and you have just narrowed it down your chance of getting the correct answer. If you really don't know, just randomly pick one choice out of the four or five choices. You'll at least have a one in four or one-in-five chance of getting it right!

3. Not Planning Your Time For Each Question

One of the many complaints by students is that there is just "not enough time" to complete certain papers. If you have done your practice papers, you'd roughly know how fast you take to complete the paper, and would have adjusted your speed from there.

However, besides from doing mock papers, students generally don't budget their time for each question well. For example, if you have a 2 hour paper, and your paper consists of three sections, you might allocate 30 minutes for the first (shorter) section, 30 minutes for the second section, and an hour for the last (longer) section, which most likely has the toughest questions which require you to take some time to think and work it out.

If you are stuck on a particular question, don't spend ten minutes brooding and thinking it over. Skip it over first and finish up on the easier questions, then come back to it later. The rule is to always keep progressing.

Note that you don't have to answer the questions by

THE A LISTER

sequence (Question 1, 2, 3, 4, ...). You can answer them in any order that you like. Just make sure that you leave enough space to write your answers when you come back to it.

4. Not reading the question fully and carefully

This one is a killer. Students lose many precious marks because they didn't read the question carefully, and hence, gave an incorrect answer which they thought was right!

If you have a tendency to be prone to careless mistakes and errors, what you need to do is to cap on your pen and put it down on the table.

Don't hold it in your hand, and don't start picking it up and writing until you are certain you have fully read and understood what the question wants from you.

Always read and re-read the question again, and highlight or underline important words in the question, such as "Define" or "NOT part of this equation".

In essence, below are some of the common instructional words and the way you should be answering them:

Describe	Explain and give relevant examples to a theorem or a concept.
State	Give the keywords or key phrases directly
List	Your keywords or key phrases in bullet points
Analyse	Take apart a concept or a process, and explain it step by step.
Discuss	Describe, explain, give examples, points for and against, then analyse and evaluate the results.
Explain	Provide a solution that gives complete details with relevant keywords for a particular question.
Define	Provide a definition

For more definitions on common instructional words used in exam questions, visit: **http://goo.gl/SE2kkc**

5. Analysis Paralysis

As a self-proclaimed "perfectionist", I tend to have trouble with this many times. If I am unsure of a question, I'd tend to second-guess my answers after I written them down and either make it better or change it entirely.

It's easy for students to fall into this trap of overthinking a question and wonder whether it is a trick question or whether your keywords are correct. My advice to you is to follow your first instinct, your gut answer. And then move on to the next question.

6. Poor spelling and grammar

For students weaker in spelling and grammar, you may tend to make mistakes in writing technical terms or writing your answer such that the marker is not able to understand it. There is not much you can do at this stage to brush up on your English, however, one tip is to write as simply as you can.

If you're weak in word construction, just answer the question as direct as you can. Also, make sure you look through your script once more and check if you've misspelt any technical terms. You can get away with misspelling other common English words, but when it comes to technical terms, make sure you've got it nailed down in your memory, as a wrong spelling might cost you some marks.

7. Writing too much or too little

On the question of how much to write, your best bet is to look at the marks allocated for that particular question. You will know that you need just a one liner or a short sentence when the marks given is only 1 or 2. And, for a bounty of five marks, you'd be expected to write a paragraph which contains around five keywords that will score you your marks.

THE A LISTER

Avoiding Post-Mortems

It's official. You've successfully survived the paper. Congrats for making it out alive! By this time, students would be chatting amongst themselves and comparing answers with each other.

Sometimes, we tend to get varying answers and we'll go into analysing mode – thinking how your paper will go wrong and mentally preparing for the worst.

There is no point engaging in such mental work, because the exam is already over – you can't change anything. If you know you have fallen short on certain parts (eg. Not being able to complete the paper on time, making an obvious careless mistake), don't beat yourself up. Pat yourself on the back for having survived the paper and learn from your mistakes, and then don't brood over it any longer, especially if you have a paper on the next day!

THE A LISTER

Activity: Becoming A Top Athlete

Becoming a top athlete means prepping yourself up to be in your best state of mind and body. In this activity, you're going to be creating your very own exam ritual that you'll execute right before any major test or exam.

In the blank spaces below, write a brief description of what you will do the night before the exam, the morning of the exam, and just before the exam.

1)   Night Before Exam

(e.g. Sleeping before 11pm, revision of mindmaps, doing one final mock paper, etc...)

_____

_____

2)   Morning of Exam Day

(e.g. Make sure stationery pouch is packed, reach 30 mins early, have a brain food filled breakfast, etc...)

_____

_____

3) Just Before Exam

(e.g. Being alone, listening to a 3-minute relaxation audio track in the washroom, 1-min visualization, affirming myself with "[insert affirmation]", etc...)

_____

_____

_____

The night before your exam or test, implement your ritual. You'll find that you feel totally different and in control of everything. By the time you begin the exam, you'll be "in the zone" for success!

THE A LISTER

STRATEGY #10

Your Most Powerful Tool...

"Whether you think you can or think you can't, either way you're right"

- Henry Ford,
Founder of Ford Motor Company

We've now arrived at the final strategy for being an 'A' Lister. I know for a fact that you have the ability to score your 'A's because you KNOW where you stand right now, and have read this book all the way because you want to improve your grades. So many people don't even complete the first ten pages of any book they read! As compared to other people who don't take an interest in wanting to improve, you are already in the lead! For that, give yourself a pat on the back.

The Next Einstein

We all have this one very powerful PC between our ears, even more powerful than any gaming PC or supercomputer.

That's right, it's our brain!

You already have everything you require inside of your brain to score 'A's on ALL your exams and become a top scorer in your school.

Don't believe it?

Look at Albert Einstein, whom we all know as the world's Mathematical genius and an insanely smart guy. However, did you know that way back when he was a teenager in school, his teachers actually labelled him as "average"?

Einstein didn't beat himself up just because his teachers said those words to him. He knew in his mind he could achieve great things, despite what others say about him. He believed in himself, and went on to become the person who he is remembered by today.

We all have the same white matter in our heads as people whom we term as intelligent like Albert Einstein, President Barack Obama, Stephen Hawking, da Vinci and Garry Kasparov have in theirs. They are no different from us, except for the fact that they understand the power of the mind.

Don't be limited by labels and people telling you that you "can never make it", that "you are better off working than studying" and that "you need to struggle in order to have a bright future". In the end, it's all about what you put into your head and what you believe in.

I believe everything created, every success or every failure, begins first in the mind. Therefore, you have to especially take care of what goes on in your mind. Feed your mind with the right stuff that leads to success.

Garbage in, garbage out.

THE A LISTER

Think of your mind as fertile garden with lots of plants in it. If you take care of it every single day, water it and fertilize it conscientiously, you'll always see beautiful plants and flowers in your garden. If you don't take care of it, your plants might die, weeds might start to grow and pesky insects will invade your garden.

Success is 80% Mind-set and 20% Strategy

You've learnt the skills of mastering your memory, setting goals, building mind-maps, critical thinking, and cutting-edge techniques to answering complex exam questions and preparing yourself for exam success. Hooray!

However, all of that will not give you significant success if you don't have this – the mindset, attitude and beliefs of success.

It's all about the white matter that's in your heads that makes the difference between a successful person and a not so successful one.

So, is your mindset tuned to attract success? Or do you have many limiting beliefs that stop you from getting where you want to go? Let's find out...

What Are The Words You Tell Yourself Every Day?

There's a famous saying that "What you think about, you bring about." If you think that you cannot do something, you will certainly find so many evidences to support that thought. In the process, you reinforce your beliefs because you SEE the results just as you expected it to be. It ultimately becomes a vicious cycle that you do not even realize has formed!

All beliefs, useful or not useful, originate from your thoughts being replayed over and over in your head.

Here are some common limiting beliefs that majority of students will have sometimes. Do you identify with any of these?

	Limiting Belief
1	I don't have a good memory.
2	I will get bored when I study. / I will fall asleep when I study
3	Studying is a waste of my time.
4	I can't do this.
5	My lecturers are lousy.
6	It's difficult to get into a University.
7	I can't achieve much in my studies.
8	I am too lazy to study.
9	There is no time
10	I'm too stressed
11	School is boring.
12	My grades are already this bad. It's no use.
13	Mistakes / Failures are bad.
14	I'm too poor to afford a tutor, so my grades suffered.
15	I always score badly at tests

THE A LISTER

You aren't born with those beliefs. They are there in your mind because of many of them had been repeated to you over and over again, either by a parent, a friend or even yourself!

One day, while I was chatting with a dear friend of mine over coffee at Starbucks, I mentioned to him casually that I was "always so stressed", "had an anxious personality" and was at my wits' end about managing my stress.

He then replied with a statement that totally blew me away. He said, "If you keep telling yourself that you have an anxious personality and is always stressed, then you WILL be stressed. You are only stressed if you THINK and BELIEVE you are stressed."

THE EAGLE WHO COULDN'T FLY

An eagle's egg was mistakenly placed in the nest of a prairie chicken one day. Over the course of a few days, the egg hatched and the little eagle grew up thinking it was a prairie chicken. After all, his siblings were all prairie chickens.

The eagle did what all the other prairie chickens did. It scratched in the dirt for seeds. It clucked and cackled. The eagle did not fly more than a few feet as that was what the other chickens did.

One day, he saw a gorgeous white eagle flying gracefully and majestically in the open sky. He asked the prairie chickens, "What is that beautiful bird?"

The chickens replied, "That is an eagle. He is an outstanding bird, but you cannot fly like him because you are just a prairie chicken."

So the eagle never gave it a second thought, believing that it was the truth. He eventually died a prairie chicken, never knowing of the fact that he was an eagle and had the glorious potential to fly.

Never let other people tell you what you are. Never identify yourself as anything less than what you are really capable of, even if it seems like you're not making any progress. So, if your inner voice tells you that you couldn't achieve the results others are achieving, make a firm resolution to show them who's boss.

Beliefs aren't truth. **YOU** make them truths by finding evidences over and over again to support those beliefs.

To escape from your limiting beliefs, you must first be aware that you are having those beliefs. Then, don't give those beliefs any power or attention. One of the ways to do this is to form new, opposing beliefs. When you focus on owning your new beliefs and giving less attention to your old ones, you start to release those unwanted beliefs.

In the following exercise, I have included a 3-step process for you to release your old beliefs and help you identify with new, positive ones:

THE A LISTER

1. **Write Down Your Top 3 Limiting Beliefs That You Think Are Stopping You From Getting the Results You Want**

   _____

   _____

   _____

2. **Ask Yourself If They Are Really True**

Sometimes, you just can't believe what you think. As humans, it's our nature to make assumptions and conclusions all the time.

But, are they all certainly true?

Most likely not. Challenge those thoughts and conclusions that you have made, ask yourself are they fact or your own opinions, and you'll find many evidences to oppose the limiting belief.

If your limiting belief is "I have no time", look around and notice those students who work hard, achieve great grades, and yet still have time to relax and go out with their friends. If your limiting belief is "I always score badly at [subject]", look at the times when you've scored well in that subject, even if it's a small test or quiz.

3. **Take Action To Disprove The Belief**

One of the quickest and most powerful ways to stop your limiting beliefs is to see and experience first-hand, you doing the "impossible". No matter how fearful or how uncomfortable it may be, you'll feel a lot differently once you've tried.

This book is a great example. I've always wanted to write and publish a book. Initially, I had deep rooted self-doubts like *"I'm not good enough to write about this", "Who will buy my book and listen to what I have to say?", "Writing a book is too tough and I don't have money to get published"*.

The fact that you're holding this book in your hands right now is real proof that I have done it and overcame all those beliefs.

Take massive action to break your beliefs. Implement the strategies I've detailed out in this book and focus only on the good thoughts. Don't think "I can't do it". Think **"How can I do it?"**

THE A LISTER

Activity: The Social Skydiver

You've now learned that your mind can be your greatest asset, and it can also be your greatest enemy.

Here's a really fun activity you must try if you want to see your limiting beliefs shatter right before your very eyes!

The task? Go up and talk to two people today whom you haven't met yet and get their phone numbers. Do not complete this task until you have successfully gotten both numbers in your hand.

Now your mind must be thinking, "Woah! Hold up here. I can't do that, that's crazy! People will think I'm crazy!"

Now here's your inner voice trying its very best to hold you down and keep you within your comfort zone.

If you aren't very extroverted, like I am, you will also be thinking, "I'll never be able to do this. I am too afraid. People wouldn't enjoy talking to me."

This is the limiting belief kicking in. What do you do? Shatter it.

Yes, go on. Even if you don't know what to say, just put yourself out there and make the first move. Make up a dumb reason why you would want their numbers in the first place. I can guarantee you that it isn't as scary as it seems.

If you got rejected and didn't get the number, relax and try again. Remember to have fun with this.

Write those numbers down in the blanks below.

1) _____

2) _____

When you have gotten both numbers, pat yourself on the back for a job well done. Congratulations! You've smashed those beliefs right in the head! You did what you thought was "impossible" to do.

This simple activity demonstrates how easy it is to get caught up in our heads and how those beliefs restrain us from accomplishing something amazing.

How did you feel after the activity? You felt awesome, didn't you?

When you start shattering the barriers to your success, you begin to become inspired in your learning, and that will propel you high up to becoming an 'A' Lister.

So, whenever you catch your mind telling you all those limiting statements, remember this activity and "*just do it*".

THE A LISTER

Being HUNGRY!!!

If you want to accelerate your grades and become an 'A' Lister, you need to be HUNGRY for success! Always dream big and take big actions. The highly successful people in life never dream small.

What drives or motivates a person is ultimately their "why". This is why I've been emphasizing on defining a strong motivation or purpose in your academic journey and staying true to that "why".

If your "why" is strong enough, you'll naturally be super hungry to achieve that "why" and take massive action to change your circumstances to bring you there.

Nothing is impossible in life. In the past, people laughed at the Wright Brothers when they talked about their dreams of being able to fly the skies. In the past, no one believed that you could store music, take pictures, write notes, read articles and play games all with a small object that fits snuggly in your hand.

So, don't care about the naysayers. Be hungry. Be daring.

No One Said It Would Be Easy

The strategies I've laid out in this book is a blueprint for skyrocketing your grades. However, just like any other success, you need to take action to see results for yourself. I can prescribe you the medicine, but you'll have to ultimately take the pills yourself. The steps are simple, but not easy.

AFTERNOTES

There you have it. Ten amazing strategies you can immediately start using to change your results and become an 'A' Lister!

I hope you found what I shared in this book useful to you, not only in your studies, but also in helping you blaze a life of your dreams. All success is attracted using the same set of principles, the same mindset and similar beliefs.

This may be the end of the book, but it's just the beginning of your path to being an 'A' Lister! Don't just stop here. Knowing and doing are two totally different things. Massively implement the strategies I've given you here. Just like how you will not become slimmer merely by watching a workout video, you will not get those 'A's you always wanted just by reading this book.

Take massive action to see massive results! Celebrate when you've achieved a little success, don't give up, and most importantly, have fun with it!

Thanks for sticking it out with me through this book. Please leave a nice review for me on my website **www.khinwai.com** or send me an email at **khinwai@thealisterbook.com**. I'd love to hear how this book has motivated or helped you in your studies. To end off, I'd like to share with you my favourite quote by Napoleon Hill:

"What the mind can conceive and believe, it can achieve."

Online Resources & Recommended Reads

Being an 'A' Lister means being super-duper resourceful in your project research, classroom assignments, and overall learning. In this section, I provide you with online resources that have helped me in my own studies, and hopefully, it will for you as well!

Mobile Study Apps

- **Wunderlist**
  - www.wunderlist.com

- **Evernote**
  - www.evernote.com

- **Google Drive**
  - www.google.com/drive

- **myHomework Student Planner**
  - www.myhomeworkapp.com

- **StudyBlue Flashcards**
  - www.studyblue.com/online-flashcards

- **EverNote Peek (for iPad)**
  - www.evernote.com/peek

- **Notability (only for iOS)**
  - www.gingerlabs.com

THE A LISTER

- **Dictionary.com Mobile**
  - www.dictionary.reference.com/apps
- **Quizlet Mobile**
  - https://quizlet.com/mobile

Online Student Resources & Websites

- **Khan Academy**
  - www.khanacademy.org
- **CliffsNotes**
  - www.cliffsnotes.com
- **Wolfram Alpha**
  - www.wolframalpha.com
- **TED**
  - http://www.ted.com
- **SparkNotes**
  - www.sparknotes.com
- **Study Guides & Strategies**
  - www.studygs.net
- **HowToStudy.org**
  - www.howtostudy.org/resources.php
- **Grade Saver**
  - www.gradesaver.com

- **Cramberry**
  - https://cramberry.net

Memory Recall Tools

- **Mindmeister**
  - www.mindmeister.com
- **XMind**
  - www.xmind.net
- **Memoria Technica**
  - www.eudesign.com/mnems/_mnframe.htm
- **Wikipedia Mnemonics**
  - http://en.wikipedia.org/wiki/Category:Mnemonics
- **Spacefem's Mnemonic Generator**
  - http://spacefem.com/mnemonics
- **JogLab's Wordfinder Tool**
  - www.joglab.com/wordfinder.htm

Productivity Tools

- **RescueTime**
  - www.rescuetime.com
- **SleepTimer**
  - http://steppschuh.net/blog/?p=299
- **Dragon Speech Recognition Software**
  - www.nuance.com/dragon/index.htm

THE A LISTER

- **SelfControl**
  - http://selfcontrolapp.com

Recommended Books

- **"I Am Gifted, So Are You" by Adam Khoo**
  - http://amzn.to/1B4Twzm

- **"The Happy Student: 5 Steps to Academic Fulfillment and Success" by Daniel Wong**
  - http://amzn.to/1z4tsZT

- **"Use Your Head" by Tony Buzan**
  - http://amzn.to/1z4A9Lv

- **"The 7 Habits of Highly Effective Teens" by Sean Covey**
  - http://amzn.to/1EFGhsA

- **Get The Best Grades With the Least Amount of Effort (eBook)**
  - http://tinyurl.com/courseone

- **The Study Method (eBook)**
  - http://tinyurl.com/coursetwo

About The Author

Ho Khinwai is one of the youngest local authors to put his pen down on the subject of getting good grades in school. He has authored his first book at age 20 while serving his National Service.

Once an average student in his Secondary School, Khinwai uses the strategies that he shares today to propel himself to the top 1% in Nanyang Polytechnic's (NYP) Business School and topped his cohort for his course, the Diploma in Banking & Finance. He has since received an undergraduate scholarship from the National University of Singapore. He was also placed on the Directors' List every consecutive semester for his outstanding academic achievements.

Khinwai is not only a published author and writer, he is a well-known young investor and infopreneur within his community.

With a desire to find out what makes ordinary people extraordinary, Khinwai had personally trained under many top gurus including Adam Khoo, Executive Chairman of Adam Khoo Learning Technologies Group (AKLTG), Mary Buffett, former daughter-in-law to billionaire Warren Buffett, JT Foxx, the World's #1 Wealth Coach and serial entrepreneur, Peng Joon, Asia's leading internet marketer, and many more. He has also personally interviewed many success icons such as Boyce Avenue, Wong Fu Productions and Ryan Higa (Nigahiga).

THE A LISTER

Currently, Khinwai is the founder of Zen Invest Solutions, which creates educational products and services that enable people to learn essential life and business skills in a simple and straightforward way.

He believes that every individual can find success in their own lives, as long as the desire for it is present and massive action is taken.

Follow Ho Khinwai at **www.khinwai.com**

www.ingramcontent.com/pod-product-compliance
Lightning Source LLC
Chambersburg PA
CBHW071505150426
43191CB00009B/1417